THE ART OF
POLE FISHING

Dickie Carr

Beekay Publishers

Other angling titles by Beekay Publishers:

Coarse

Carp Fever by Kevin Maddocks
Pike Fishing in the 80's by Neville Fickling
Basic Carp Fishing by Peter Mohan
Modern Specimen Hunting by Jim Gibbinson
Top Ten – tactics for the major species from ten leading anglers.
Edited by Bruce Vaughan
Redmire Pool by Kevin Clifford & Len Arbery
Tactics for Big Pike by Bill Chillingworth
In Pursuit of Carp & Catfish by Kevin Maddocks
Cypry The Carp by Peter Mohan
The Beekay Guide to 450 Carp Waters
Jim Davidson Gets Hooked by Jim Davidson
In Pursuit of Predatory Fish by Neville Fickling
Tiger Bay by Rob Maylin
Understanding Barbel by Fred Crouch
Big-Water Carp by Jim Gibbinson
Mega-Pike by Eddie Turner

Sea

Boat Fishing at Sea by Phill Williams & Brian Douglas
Long Range Casting & Fishing Techniques by Paul Kerry
Cod Fishing by John Rawle
Uptide & Boatcasting by Bob Cox

Game

The Colour Guide to Fly Tying by Kevin Hyatt
Robson's Guide to Stillwater Trout Flies by Kenneth Robson
Dressed to Kill by Bob Carnill & Kenneth Robson
(For further details write to Beekay for a free catalogue)

First published in 1990 by
BEEKAY PUBLISHERS
WITHY POOL, BEDFORD ROAD,
HENLOW CAMP, BEDS. SG16 6EA
© Beekay Publishers 1990

ISBN 0 947674 35 7

Typeset by BP Integraphics Ltd., Bath, Avon

Printed in Great Britain at The Bath Press, Avon

Contents

Acknowledgements

I want to take this opportunity to thank all those who have helped with the production of this book, and especially my friends and fellow match anglers Richard Borley, Peter Burrell and Mick Burrell for their valuable contributions to the book; Alan Whibley for his excellent drawings; Kevin Maddocks of Beekay Publishers for all his help and encouragement and for organising and obtaining the photographs and line drawings; Don Neish of Don's of Edmonton, and Jack Simpson of Simpsons of Turnford, for their help with technical information and ideas; Roger Hurst, the Simpsons rod builder, who makes all my rods for me, Bait 78 for kindly supplying groundbaits; and John Baker, Bruce Vaughan, Mick Thill, Rodney Coldron and Dave Harper for providing the pictures.

Without the assistance of all these people, this book would never have been published, and I am truly grateful to them and also to all my friends and colleagues on the match angling circuit who, perhaps unknowingly, have contributed to the knowledge I have gained of pole fishing, and which I have put into this book.

History of Pole Fishing

My reason for wanting to write a book on pole fishing is that there seems to be a great increase of interest in the subject, so it is the right time for a book on the pole by someone who has had some success with the method at national level. For some time Jack Simpson's of Turnford, who build and market my rods, has urged me to write a book, and at the many forums and meetings I attend I am often asked for a good book on pole fishing. My mail also contains many letters on the subject.

My intention is to write a simple account of how to use the pole successfully, which can be bought for a small extra cost by anyone setting up as a pole angler, along with the basic tackle he will need. I hope also to include enough information for the book to be useful to more experienced anglers as well, who would like to improve their performance when using the pole, particularly in matches.

Since I live in the River Lea area, I like to think that I am carrying on a tradition as a pole angler, because for a long time the Lea Valley was the home of pole fishing. In my own time I learnt much as a youngster while I was a member of the King's Arms and Eastern Enfield angling clubs from such local pole experts as Charlie Hatt, Fred Chapman, Reg Matthews, Jack White, Jack Meads and Edgar Fisher. In the 50's and 60's we youngsters used to sit on tackle boxes in the King's Arms coach on the way to the outings and matches, and listen to the experts who occupied the booked seats, ninety per cent of whom used the pole.

However, the history of the pole or roach-pole, as it was then called, goes back long before this. Before reels were invented, anglers used to tie their line onto the ends of their rods, or poles, and it didn't take long to learn that the longer the pole they could hold, the more control they had over their end tackle. In that angling classic of the 30's 'Angling Ways', by Eric Marshall-Hardy, published in 1934, the roach pole only gets a brief mention, but it is a revealing one: 'The finest exponents of "swimming the stream" are possibly the old school of roach pole anglers, a mode of fishing which appears to be waning in and around London, where its best exponents have always been found. This may be due to the fact that the lightest roach pole is a heavy and cumbersome affair compared with Nottingham and Sheffield rods. The poles vary in length from 14 to 18 feet, and are gently tapered from the butt to the pole tip ... no reel is used in this type of fishing, the cast and hook link being attached to a short length of line known as "topping" which in turn is tied to a ring at the tip of the rod. ... Some of the Lea experts use the finest possible tackle, and it is not uncommon for them to land a hefty chub when fishing for dace, or a barbel weighing four or five pounds, when they had not expected anything larger than a half pound roach. ... The pole tip is not more than two feet from the float. ... When a long roach pole is being used, it is sometimes difficult to bring a fish sufficiently near to net it; in this case the butt and sometimes the second joint is unshipped.'

The use of the pole may have been 'waning' in the early 30's, but the reverse is the case at present. I am often asked why, and also why the Continental angler seems to be more successful with the modern pole than his English counterpart; after all, World Championships have all been won with the pole and the English have not been winning any of them until recently. In my opinion this is because while English anglers went on to diversify their fishing methods, using shorter rods, and reels, in the Nottingham and Sheffield styles, as Marshall-Hardy goes on to relate in his book in the section after the one quoted, anglers on the Continent tended to concentrate on improving their pole fishing techniques, which led them to develop the longer and lighter poles of today.

Most of the early roach poles were made by Sowerbutts, and were bored-out cane with heavy brass ferrules. They were all of the take-apart type, of course, with no elastic used, and the line tied to the tip ring. Peacock, pheasant and crow quills were the main types of floats used with the poles, and as there were no shot at that time, home-made leads were used as weights. Bread, worms and caddis were the main baits. We started with thin light cheap poles made in Japan, which cost about ten shillings (50p) in 1960. The tip was as thin as a modern quiver tip, which was excellent for playing fish. Two to four feet of line above the float only was used, and the joints were taken off one at a time to land the fish. Line was usually plaited silk with silkworm gut and later gut substitute for the casts.

The name 'Roach Pole' originated because the rivers of the past were filled with roach, and perhaps 90% of the fish caught were roach. The bream were often further out and so were not caught on the pole, while as the bait was lowered straight down, the roach got the bait before the shallower swimming bleak. Heavier lines were used than those of today, breaking strains of three and four pounds being common. Barbed hooks, both eyed and spade ends, were used, and the sizes were much bigger than we use now, mostly 10's and 12's. Hemp, tares and elderberries became popular in my time as baits, and we also used home-made swim feeders. Float ledgering was often used for the bigger fish. While pole fishing continued to be popular in the south of England, the northerner got ahead with other methods using reels, which is why the earlier fishing styles were named after the more northern towns where they originated.

The revival of interest in pole fishing has come about because of the success of the Continentals, particularly the French, in winning world championships with the pole method. It could soon be seen that we had dropped behind in the pole fishing techniques, which is why the English got beaten so many times in the past. The Continentals had also concentrated on bloodworm fishing techniques which have only recently become more popular in this country, so we have quite a way to go to 'catch up'. Pole fishing has proved to be best for team fishing in matches, and it is now becoming much more popular in this country both because of the successes of the Continentals and because there are now so many team events, such as the AT Winter Leagues, in which most match anglers take part. You have to work hard for bites, especially on canals where many of these events take place, and the pole is ideal for canals. Twenty years ago, around 2% of match anglers would have carried poles; now 99% have them. The pole is now the 'in' thing in match fishing; the latest craze.

Really, 'modern' pole fishing started with the introduction by Continental match anglers, some 15 to 20 years ago, of fibre glass poles, which were much lighter and had a better action than old cane poles. The English, as usual, went over rather slowly to the new material, but because of the lighter weight, much longer poles could be used, most being 24 to 26 feet in length. They were very thick, and were still heavy by today's standards. The line was still tied to the end ring, but smaller hooks and lighter lines were coming into use. The joints still fitted into each other and the poles were of the take-apart type. LAA Shield teams used these poles to good effect on the Thames in winter, often 'holding back' with crow quills, a method which is explained later in the book. In the summer hemp was often used, with bait droppers. Swinging fish to hand to save time also started to become popular—about 17 feet of line would be used with an 18ft pole. These longer fibre glass poles enabled the match angler to present his bait better and further out. Another development in modern pole fishing which occurred at about this time, was the use of elastic attached to the pole and the line to enable the angler to have more chance of landing big fish. Methods of using elastic will be described later in the book.

The next development was the use of carbon fibre. These super-light poles began to come into fashion in this country in 1978, the year after the Luxembourg World Championships when I fished in the England team on the River Moselle. We came fifth. No one in the England team used a pole longer than 27 feet, but the Continental teams were equipped with ten to eleven metre (33–36 feet) long carbon fibre poles enabling them to fish further out and over the close-in boulders, which made all the difference to the results. These new long poles were the main advantage they had over us, and the following year, when they were introduced into this country we all got the longer poles, myself included. The carbon fibre poles are lighter and thinner, and so could be used at much greater range. The prices of carbon poles are very high, the cheapest being £190. At first people couldn't afford them, but now many match anglers have three or four, including one or two costing £750 each—what a contrast to the 50p roach poles I started with! The ten to eleven metre poles made of carbon fibre are very light and thin for their length. It is easy to get your hand round them and they have a very good action.

Instead of having to take apart the pole at each section to land the fish, with the modern pole you can slide them through your hand and detach the pole at the appropriate join, which is obviously much quicker and easier.

I have no doubt that pole fishing would almost have disappeared by now without the development of the new materials, enabling the pole fisherman to fish at a greater range with lighter and easier to handle poles.

Will there be further developments? I expect there will; some rods are already being made of a new material called boron which is said to be superior to carbon fibre for building poles, so it will be interesting to see if this new material, and others, improve poles still more in the future.

Typical Pole Fishing Venues

I have been asked by quite a few people up and down the country to recommend some typical venues for pole fishing. It is impossible to give too much detail, but I will list a few good waters for pole fishing.

In the London area two good venues come to mind, the first of which, Dartford Lakes in Kent, is a great pole water. This is a very good water in summer using hemp and casters for roach fishing. Day tickets are available on the water, but no keep nets are allowed—an ideal practice water. On the other side of London, Stanborough Lake, Welwyn Garden City, Herts is good on the pole for skimmer bream and roach, using hemp, caster and small red worms for the bream. Day tickets are available on the bank; groundbait and keep nets are banned. All the forest ponds around London are well worth trying; they are full of fish and the scenery and the countryside are very pleasant. Thames Water Authority licences are needed for all these waters. In other parts of the country there are a number of good waters, but you will need to enquire locally about permits. Some of these are: Rudyard Lake, Cheshire, an

Dickie with 50–15 at the Sankey Invitation Championship at Longleat, just one of his many victories.

ideal place to learn pole fishing with bloodworm; Pilsworth Reservoir, Leigh, Manchester, a good bloodworm water; Worsborough Reservoir, Barnsley, Yorkshire, which is often used for practice by the well known Barnsley Blacks match team; in East Anglia, Barnham Pits, Ipswich, Suffolk, are solid with fish and well worth a visit for pole practice, whilst in the Birmingham area Edgbaston Reservoirs are good, with plenty of roach and perch; best baits are bloodworm and bronze maggot. The Royal Military Canal, in the south east, in the Hythe area of Kent, is good and in the south west of the country the Gloucester Canal, which I have visited recently, has good pole fishing with a variety of depths, whilst in the north east the River Witham is very good for the pole and bloodworm. Obviously, I have only mentioned a few good pole waters in each area as there are so many waters where the pole can be used successfully.

How to enter matches

Newcomers to pole fishing often ask me how to get started and the following is some advice for beginners. Lists of matches are kept at some tackle shops, or buy Angling Times and Angler's Mail and look at the Match Guide, which gives entry details, telephone numbers and how to book in for a match. I recommend that you should not go onto the Open Match circuit until you have done well on local club matches. Go on the coach outings, fish in local matches, and don't start to enter the Opens until you can win the local matches.

No-one, even the most successful, makes a fortune out of the Open Match circuit; even if you win money, expenses can be very high. Whilst on the subject of expenses I should like to tell you of what happened to me when I got my fixtures mixed up and found that I was supposed to fish both an invitation match at Longleat and the Home Internationals for the South of England. The winner at Longleat would get £2,000 and my expenses would be only £30–£40, but for the Home International in Ireland there was no prize money, and it would cost me £300–£400 in expenses. However, I had promised Dennis Salmon I would fish, so I opted for the Internationl because I also felt that doing well here would help my England position and that the money side of it was not the most important. The full story of that match appears later in the book.

Types of Poles and their Fittings

There are now two types of poles—telescopic, and take-apart. When buying your first pole I would advise against getting the telescopic type. This is more of a specialist pole, so start with the take-apart type. I also suggest that after you have decided what type to buy, you should get as long a pole as you can afford. At first, if you are used to rods, the pole will seem very long, but you will be surprised how soon you get used to it, and very soon you will be wishing you had a longer one. It's like buying a car—at first your choice may seem fast but once you get used to it, you may well wish you had bought a faster one still!

Your first pole should be a fibre glass one; it will not be anything like as expensive as carbon fibre, so if you don't like pole fishing, and you want to give it up, you will not have lost too much. Buy the longest pole you can afford. I would recommend that the length should not be less than 21 feet. Remember you do not have to use the pole in its full length and it is more practicable to have length available should you need it.

When choosing your first pole try as many as you can to give you an idea of the different makes and compare the weight, action and of course the price.

As a guide I would suggest you select the lightest and stiffest pole that you can afford and as I have already mentioned, make it one of the 'take-apart' kind and not a telescopic.

I am so often asked what advantage a pole has over rod and reel fishing, and I can answer this in one word—presentation. I will now go on to give you the reasons for using each type of pole.

Take-Apart Pole. These are for fishing a short line to the float for good presentation of the bait to the fish, and for speed fishing in swinging fish to the hand. With the take-apart poles the traditional ferrules are better because the larger part fits over the top of the next section up and ensures that your hand does not catch on a shoulder of the joint when you slide it through your hands to break the pole down. If the

Don Neish and Dickie comparing carbon bleak whip poles.

pole is very stiff it is harder to cast the tackle out, and heavier tackle may be needed.

Carbon Fibre Poles. Carbon fibre poles are the same as the take-apart poles, only they are lighter and are used for fishing at longer distances than the fibre glass poles.

Telescopic Poles. The telescopic pole is more often used for smaller fish and is normally used with a length of line slightly shorter than the length of the pole—say one to two feet shorter, because these poles are floppy, and the bend in the pole must be allowed for. These telescopic poles are very good as 'bleak whips' and when taking fish from the surface or in shallow water. I have seen members of the Italian World Championship team using telescopic poles eight or nine metres long, with the line 18 inches shorter than the pole. They flick the float out underarm, moving the pole with the float through the swim, and catching very fast.

It is a good idea to plug the pole joints with polystyrene or foam at the thicker end, so that if you should drop the section into the water, it will sink more slowly, and you may have time to retrieve it.

When dismantling the pole put the sections pointing upwards behind you so that they rest on something and do not lie flat on the ground. Ensure that your pole joints are kept clean, as mud and grit can easily damage them.

New Poles

At the moment we are spoilt for selection of poles, with poles now up to 14 metres, so that people can fish on the far side of canals; it makes you wonder when it's going to come to an end! The improvement in poles over the last two or three years has been incredible. They seem to get longer, lighter and stiffer! I will just try to mention a few of the most popular new poles of today.

I think that Tri-Anna are one of the outstanding poles, and I now have one with my name on it made by Tri-Anna, which without advertising, I would say is very good value for money. It sells from about £500 at 11 metres, and it is very light and easy to use.

Also Browning have a very good range of poles in all price brackets and Lifeam and Maver have a very good pole in the Lifeum, and another I feel I must mention is the new Daiwa pole, which does sell for over £1,000, but I've heard very good reports about it. Other good names in poles are Silstar and Olympic.

Now that I have finished discussing the types of poles, I will answer one of the questions I get asked most; that is, how the lines and elastic should be attached to the poles. I will start with the *flick-tip*, which is a fine and flexible top joint very much like a quiver tip. This is used mainly for fishing for small fish, and without elastic. I have found it best to affix the line to the end of the tip in the following manner; I whip a wire float eye to the 'quiver tip' about a quarter of an inch from the end. I then put a loop in the end of the line and pass the loop through the eye, and over the end of the pole. This should then be pulled tight. A small piece of silicone rubber tube is then put over the quiver tip and is slid over the eye so that it is covered. This helps to prevent it from slipping.

The Crook. This is the commonest method of attaching the shock elastic to a pole. There are basically two types of pole crooks. The continental style crooks are made in various sizes to fit either over or into the next section down from the tip; in other words the tip is not used.

Many newcomers to pole fishing find it difficult to accept that you discard what, on first impression is such a vital part of their pole. Remember however that the crook and elastic absorber are being used to give you greater insurance against breakage should you hook larger fish. They do in fact take the place of the tip of the rod.

There are also crooks which are fitted by cutting back the top until they actually fit the top of the pole.

Remember, however, that a crook which is fitted to a very soft section can cause tangles. If you are in doubt go to a good tackle shop which stocks pole tackle and seek their advice.

To attach the elastic to the crook, put a loop in the end of the

METHOD OF ATTACHING LINE TO END OF POLE

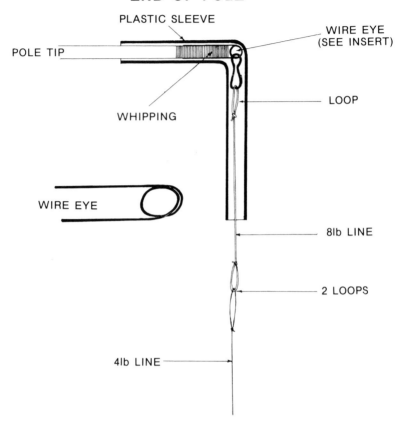

elastic and fit it round the slot provided on the crook. Push the plastic sleeve on the crook over the slot to hold the line.

One piece of good advice on the use of elastic is to keep it at least 14–20 inches in length. There will then be fewer tangles than if you had used a shorter length of elastic, and of course you will have more chance of landing bigger fish because there will be more stretch in the elastic to absorb the shock caused by the force of the fish's pull.

There are two other types of crooks. The first type has a screw fitting. The pole is cut back in the same way as used for the push-in type and the crook is screwed into the tip. The larger sort of crook has a length

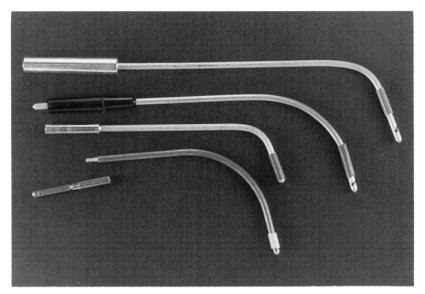

This photograph shows a varied selection of pole crooks.

of elastic inside the hollow part of the crook, and this protrudes from the end. The purpose of the crook is to divide the line from the pole so that the line does not tangle round it. This means that the best crooks to buy are the ones with the longest 'drop', don't get the long crooks with a small drop. Some of the modern crooks are much lighter so you will not need to cut much off the pole when you are fitting them.

Now we come to the method of fishing where the elastic is fitted inside the top three sections of the pole. Araldite a plastic ferrule or ring into the tip of the pole, and through this ring thread a length of heavy line, to which you have attached a swivel. Half way down the three sections the other end of the line is attached to three or four feet of elastic, and this is fixed to a piece of cork. Put a hole through the cork for the elastic and then put a bead onto the elastic to prevent it from pulling through the cork. The cork is then fitted into the end of the section of the pole.

A good tip is to put some washing-up liquid round the end ring to make the line slide more easily. This is particularly useful when you are likely to be playing big fish.

The second method of attaching elastic is the one I like best, and was invented by Mick Burrell. About a foot from the tip a small eye is whipped onto the pole. Just over another foot down the pole a line winder is whipped onto the pole, at the top of the second joint, and

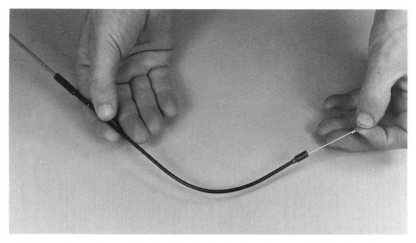

Pole crooks can be purchased with the elastic already internally fitted as shown here.

ELASTIC THROUGH CENTRE TYPE FIXING
(TOP 3 JOINTS OF POLE)

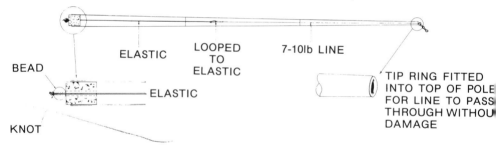

ELASTIC

LOOPED TO ELASTIC

7-10lb LINE

BEAD

ELASTIC

TIP RING FITTED INTO TOP OF POLE FOR LINE TO PASS THROUGH WITHOUT DAMAGE

KNOT

a length of line of about five yards is wound round the winder. This line is then attached to a swivel which is itself fixed to the end of a piece of elastic by means of a loop. The elastic in this case should be 14 to 15 inches long, and should be attached to a loop whipped onto the fourth section of the pole. The elastic is also threaded through a small eye placed a foot from the end of the elastic. If more line is needed while you are fishing, it can be unwound from the winder; if less line

MICK BURRELL TYPE FIXING OF ELASTIC
(TOP 4 JOINTS OF POLE)

SHOT

12 + ″   6″   12″

SWIVEL   1-7lb LINE   NOTE: SHOT IS FITTED
                                    AT TIP AFTER TENSION
HEAVY ELASTIC ATTACHED   IS ATTAINED
TO EYE, THROUGH NEXT EYE   LINE WINDER
& ATTACHED TO SWIVEL,   SEVERAL COILS OF
VIA LOOP BOTH ENDS   LINE; 2 YARDS

is required, this process can be reversed. To keep a bit of tension on the elastic a shot is placed on the line by the tip ring. The major advantage of this method is that you do not sacrifice any of your tip so that you can fish with the sensitivity of the pole's built in flick tip for small fish and still have the advantage of the elastic should you hook a bigger fish.

Pole Fishing Accessories

Most pole fishing is done with lines of $1\frac{1}{2}$ to $2\frac{1}{2}$ pounds breaking strain, but you will need to buy lines of 8 ounces, 12 ounces and 1 pound breaking strain. Heavier lines should be carried but would not normally be used except in Ireland. (Pole fishing in Ireland will be dealt with later in the book.)

The make of line used is a personal choice, but I use Efgeeco or Bayer. I also like Garbolino line, and Racing Tortue is good. For hook lengths I prefer Don's Match Special, which is certainly the best line at 12 ounces breaking strain. It is best to take no notice of the manufacturer's quoted breaking strains for lines, as they will be found to vary. Test them yourself by knotting the line with the knots you will be fishing with, and testing the breaking strain on a spring balance. The suppleness of line may make a difference to the number of takes you get. You can test for suppleness by placing pieces of line of exactly the same length over a ruler, and weighting them with a shot at the end. The weight of the shot on each piece of line must be the same. Look at the angle of droop over the ruler; the stiffest line will droop least, and the more supple line will show the biggest angle of droop. Many anglers make the mistake of choosing their nylon solely on diameter. Remember a soft, supple nylon will give you better presentation and therefore more bites.

Since there is no difference in the density of nylon lines, whether they sink or float depends on the dressing used by the manufacturer. If this is likely to matter, test the lines for floating properties before using them.

I prefer lines with some stretch, and, as I have already said, I find Efgeeco and Don's of Edmonton lines the best.

To compare the diameter of lines, wrap equal numbers of turns of line round a pin. Then compare the length of the coils to find out which line has the least diameter. This way you can find which line gives you most suppleness, the required strength and least thickness.

Now I come to hooks. I use different types of hooks for different types of fishing, and I will list these and what I use them for.

5713 Mustad. This is a barbed hook, and I only use barbed hooks when I am using a take-apart pole. This hook is the best for small fish and for bloodworm, pinkie and squatt fishing.

5715 Mustad. This is the same as the 5713 but it is barbless, and is, in my opinion, the best hook in the market for small fish bloodworm fishing. Little trouble is experienced with the points of these hooks, and they can normally be used for a five hour match without it being necessary to change the hook.

270S Mustad. This is a crystal flatted blued hook with an extra long shank and is very good for caster fishing.

313 Mustad. This used to be one of the most popular hooks for pole fishing, and one which I have always liked for casters. It does now seem to have deteriorated a bit in quality in some batches, and the barbs may not be reliable in the new hooks and may also stick out too much. I like the *Au Lion D'or 'Special Concours'* (barbed) for fishing with bigger maggots on take-apart poles and also for the larger maggots I recommend the Au Lion D'or 1219 B (barbless), which is a good hook for catching reasonable sized fish on the pole. Another hook I like for maggot fishing is the 90340 barbless. The last personal preference hook I advise is the *39855 Mustad.* This hook is barbed but I squeeze down the barb for speed fishing. I like to use this hook in Northern Ireland when I am after large bags of fish of 100 pounds plus. This hook, with the *39855 Mustad,* is the one most commonly used for bream fishing, with the bomb. Other hooks I sometimes use are:

8408 VMC—a very strong hook; 1207 *Au Lion D'or;* and for swim feeder fishing the *Mustad B53* (barbless), which is a very good sharp, strong hook recommended for feeder fishing for chub on the Thames and similar rivers. It may sometimes pay to colour the shanks of the hooks the same colour as the bait, and longer shanks for extra strength are also worth considering. A good way to store hooks is to line a box with foam, and store them according to whether the hooks appear to have sharper points, or less sharp points. They can be graded in the box according to the type of hook they are, although you will need to find this out by close examination of every hook in each batch, as there are considerable variations in all batches of hooks you buy. A strong magnifying glass to examine the hook points will be useful.

The Palomar knot is best for eyed hooks, and you will see that both types of knots to be used for tying on hooks are illustrated.

Shot

Olivettes are commonly used with the pole, and are made in various sizes from No. 1 to No. 11. The highest number is the heaviest weight at three grams, while the number 1 weighs approximately 0.2 grams.

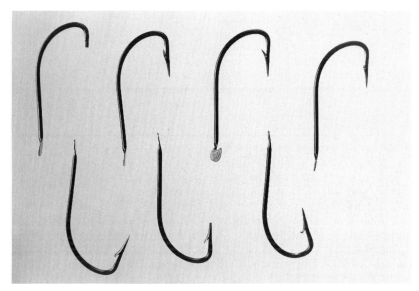

These are all hooks rejected by Dickie after inspection with a magnifying glass. These are size 22 and the naked eye could miss such faults.

These weights were invented by the French for serious pole fishing. Their advantages are that they are virtually tangle free, they look neat, and when using them in the summer for hemp and caster fishing for roach you don't get 'shot bites'. Be warned that the size of Olivettes vary according to the brand, so specify the brand name when buying them. Olivettes are normally placed on the line with the thick end down, but at times it might be better to reverse them to lessen resistance as they fall through the water and to avoid tangles.

Split Shot

For serious pole fishing you will need shots down to No. 13's although I would advise buying a complete range of shot and also 'mouse droppings' and lead wire, the uses of which I will describe later. Most people carry too much shot, and in these days when anglers are under fire for damaging wild life with discarded shot, it is a good idea to make sure you lose as little as possible. If you prepare an 'adhesive stick' using, for example, the type of sticky pads which are used to attach photographs to paper, you can stick the shot on this. The larger shot can be at one end, with the smaller at the other. If you make sure that the slit in the shot is

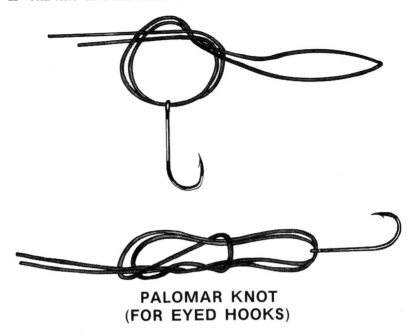

PALOMAR KNOT
(FOR EYED HOOKS)

1. DOUBLE ABOUT 4″ LINE AND PASS THROUGH EYE OF HOOK.
2. LET HOOK HANG LOOSE AND TIE OVERHAND KNOT IN DOUBLED LINE — AVOID TWISTING THE LINES AND DO NOT TIGHTEN KNOT.
3. PULL LOOP OF LINE FAR ENOUGH TO PASS IT OVER HOOK, MAKING SURE LOOP PASSES COMPLETELY OVER.
4. PULL BOTH TAG ENDS AND STANDING LINE TO TIGHTEN.

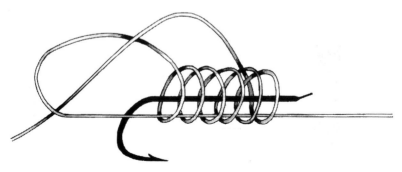

WHIPPING KNOT FOR SPADE END HOOKS

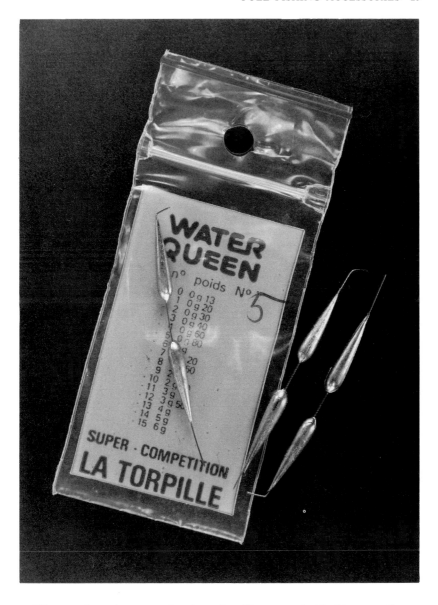

Olivettes—shown here as purchased on wires. They are packed in this way so that the holes remain clear and ready for use.

facing outwards, the shot can be attached to the line by just draping the line across the split while the shot is still attached to the adhesive, and then pinching the shot onto the line. Half an ounce or so of shot can be carried in this way and they will not get split easily.

Floats

I prefer to leave detailed advice on floats to a later section of the book, which will include detailed diagrams of all floats used with the pole, and advice on what to buy.

Winders

These come in various sizes and colours and I prefer to get long ones so that no floats stick out from the end of the winders to get damaged. What I like to do with winders is to fix a piece of tape on the side of each and to write on it the length of the line, size of the hook, and the breaking strain of the line, so you know exactly what you are putting on.

I have now given details of all the basic tackle needed for pole fishing, but other useful accessories are:

Cardboard Hook Winders. This is a three-inch square piece of corrugated cardboard. Hook lengths, especially small ones, are prepared at home and fixed on the winder. Mark them with the breaking strain and hook size. These small hook winders take up less room than a hookboard, which is also a good idea.

The Hookboard is a larger version of the hook winder, and is made of cork of from 10 by 6 inches to 12 by 10 inches in size. It is ideal for longer hook lengths. It is also possible to buy from specialist shops different size cork hook boards. These have a fixed wire rod onto which the hook is looped; the nylon is then wound around the cork board and held firmly in place with a coloured mapping pin. Different coloured pins can be used to code your hook sizes or breaking strain hook lengths. Several different types of *plummets* should be carried, and I would advise all pole anglers to have two or three disgorgers. The blunt plastic floating ones in different colours are best. Do not use sharp, forked metal disgorgers as these can damage fish.

Rod Rests of the types shown in the diagram are those normally used for pole fishing. When using this sort of back rest, make sure you get it well into the ground to avoid it moving in strong winds.

Bait Stands. I do think that bait stands are definitely needed when pole fishing because you need everything at hand and in a comfortable position. Feeding and taking maggots from the box is so much easier

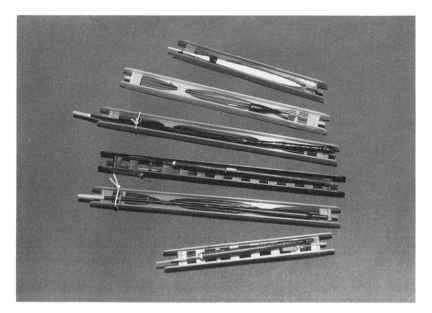

A few of Dickie's favourite pole tackles.

when you have a bait stand close beside you. It is also useful to put your plummet and disgorger on to save you having to search through your box every time you need them. I know that you can keep the disgorger on a string around your neck, but I think it is better to have it on a bait stand.

I have found that the best bait stands are those made of aluminium with holes cut into them, although this is a matter of personal preference. I also like to have a second stand on which to keep the ground bait, and I will tell you how I get the ground bait bowl on my level—to make it easier to use.

In a small washing up bowl, drill a hole in the centre of the bottom and put a $\frac{3}{8}''$ BSF bolt through this, with a washer on either side. This then screws into a bank stick, and I find it an excellent way of having a ground bait bowl ready for immediate use. Now I suppose someone will immediately want to ask what to do when fishing on concrete. To the side of my fibre glass sit-on tackle box I attach a square Tupperware bait container. This is fixed onto the tackle box with a wing nut, a system which makes it possible to get the bait easily from the container without moving from the seat.

Adjustable Legs

Adjustable legs are now on the market to fit any tackle box, and I think these are most essential for when you are pole fishing; you must be comfortable and have your box nice and even, and stable.

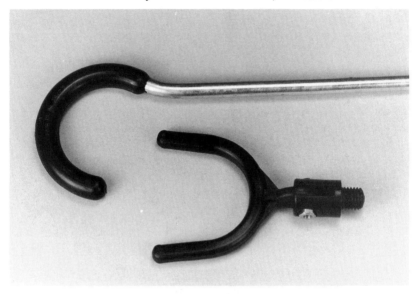

Front and rear pole rests.

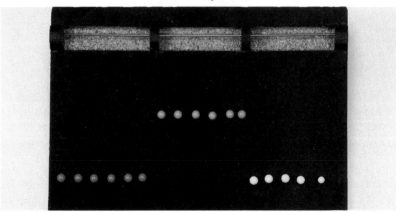

The hookboard—the hook is attached to the wire and the line wound around the board. Pins with different coloured heads are then pushed through the end loop into the board. The different breaking strain hook lengths can then be identified by a particular colour.

The pole in its rests.

The whopper dropper—one of the best catapults for the pole angler.

The all-important bait tray mounted on a bank stick and positioned close to the seat. Besides supporting a variety of baits note the other items of tackle conveniently placed, such as the disgorger, plummet, scissors, bait dropper, catapult, etc.

Baits for Pole Fishing

Casters. A caster is a maggot chrysalis, and the maggots are best turned into casters by keeping them in the fridge at approximately 32–35° Fahrenheit, where they will turn more slowly into casters. You will need plenty of slightly damp sawdust, which will help to turn a good caster. I am a great believer in fresh baits, so I recommend that old casters should never be used. The size of casters is not very important, but they MUST be fresh, and all must be sinkers both for hook baits and for throwing in as free offerings. To emphasise the importance of this, imagine that you are sitting in the cinema and eating grapes from a bag. If you put a bad one in your mouth, you will examine all the rest carefully before you eat any more. Now transfer this idea into a fishing context; if you throw in old, poor quality casters, the fish may try them, not like them, and start to reject them, including the one you have on the hook. This illustrates the importance of bait.

Once turned, the best way to keep the casters is in a bait box with some polythene over the lid. Lift the lid, and press the box to expel the air. In this way the casters will keep better. If the box is not full, put in a piece of newspaper to make it full of the casters. I never take any casters to my fishing venue in the polythene bags in which they are sold. On purchase I take them home and remove any maggot skins. Do this as quickly as possible as the longer your bait is exposed the more likely the casters will turn into floaters. Casters left in the polythene bag become 'bruised' and the maggot skins can taint the bait and make it unacceptable to the fish. I don't put the casters in the water until I get to the waterside and am ready to fish. I then add some water. If this is not done, the caster may float. Any casters which do float can be skimmed off and these can be used as hook baits.

Floating casters, if used as loose feed will drift on the surface and can take fish away from your swim. They also have the unwelcome habit of attracting unwanted water fowl to the swim which can obviously disturb your fish.

Maggots. If your wife or mother will allow it, keep your maggots in the fridge. Old fridges can be bought for a few pounds and you will

A typical caster sieve.

find that they more than repay for themselves by saving your money on bait which would otherwise deteriorate. I buy my maggots at my local tackle shop. Have a variety of colours—yellow, red and chrysodine (orange). To prepare the maggots, first run them through a sieve to get rid of the loose skins, and then add a little maize meal, which I find is very good to keep the maggots in.

Pinkies. The pinkie is a small maggot, and is a very good bait for most small fish, although bream also like them. Again a variety of colours should be used—yellow, white, chrysodine and rhodamine (red). Before I describe their use, these pinkies should be kept well away from the house, if possible; they seem to be able to escape from anything. To give you some idea of the problems this can cause, I must tell you of what happened to Jim Yeoman, a friend of mine. When he used pinkies for the first time last season, he prepared for an early start by leaving all his tackle and bait in the hall overnight. During the night the pinkies got through the holes in the box and crawled into the hall carpet. His wife was not very pleased with him when he got home, to say the least, and they had flies hatching from the carpet for the next three weeks; a lesson to all who use pinkies.

Pinkies are hard to colour, and the best method for colouring them with Rhodamine is as follows: take a small handful of very fresh pinkies, and sieve them out until they are completely clean, then put them into a bait box which has very small holes. Add about one sixteenth of an inch of water to the bottom of the box, and put the pinkies in. Sprinkle the Rhodamine powder on them and leave them overnight. Usually about 50% of the pinkies will drink the water and will become dyed with the Rhodamine. This is the only way I know to dye pinkies with Rhodamine, unless you breed them, in which case the red colour is introduced on the meat on which the pinkie is feeding, the dye is then absorbed internally into the bait from the meat which it has eaten. Such maggots are commonly called 'feed dyed'.

You will now note that the pinkies will float, and this can be a great advantage when fishing with them. The weight of the hook will just sink them, and they will sink very naturally, while on the bottom they will be counterbalanced by the weight of the hook, and will move naturally in the water.

Squatts are the smallest maggots you can buy, and are used for feeding. Both small fish and bream like these squatts, and they are a good bait in the winter or when bloodworm is barred. Squatts attract bream of all sizes. Squatts when thrown in the water tend to stay on the river or lake bed whereas pinkies and maggots are inclined to crawl away. Now and again, I do fish squatts on the hook, especially on canals or where there are very small bream. I find that the best hooks are the 7515/7513 pattern already mentioned, in size 26's. Rhodamine dyed squatts will give you an advantage if you fish them in winter, and I will tell you the only way I know of dying squatts with Rhodamine. Take a piece of sliced bread, dampen it slightly, and sprinkle the Rhodamine on the bread, and drop a small quantity of squatts on the bread. They eat the bread and are dyed, although the colour may affect only a few of the squatts. It is impossible to say how much Rhodamine should be used; you will only find this out by trial and error.

Gozzers. Now we come to gozzers which are a soft home-bred maggot. No matter what anyone says, I don't believe you can buy gozzers in the shop, so you must breed your own. They are bred on chicken, pigeon

Sieving pinkies with a fireguard sieve.

and fish; I use chicken. I will try to describe the best way of breeding gozzers. First get a piece of chicken—a leg will do, the size depending on how many gozzers you want to produce. Make sure the chicken is as dry as possible, and place it on a saucer in a shoe box, with a cut out of one corner of about an inch square. Put this at the bottom of the garden or a reasonable distance from the house. The worst enemy here is cats, which often get to the meat before the flies. The ideal time to put out the box is about two hours before dark, and if the weather is reasonably warm you should have little problem in getting 'blows'—eggs laid by flies. When the eggs have been laid, wrap the meat in newspaper, put it in a bowl, and cover it with bran to prevent the smell, which can be terrible. Experience will tell you how many eggs you need.

Gozzers can be dyed and an ideal time to put the dye in is when the maggots are about one eighth of an inch in length. The maggots are ready more quickly in warmer weather and experimentation will tell you how much dye to use, and when the maggots should be put into the fridge to slow them down. Gozzers are only soft skinned for the first 24 hours of their natural cycle. By storing them in a fridge you can prolong the period of soft skin. The best time to take them off the meat is about two days before they are needed, so that they will still

Dyeing pinkies as described in text.

have some feed inside them. The best method is to place the meat in a sieve over a bucket, when the gozzers will drop through into the bucket. They should then be put in a bait box with some damp bran, and then put straight into the fridge. The bran should be changed regularly to keep the gozzers in peak condition. Now you have gone to all this trouble to breed the gozzers, you will no doubt find people who will ask whether it is worth while. My answer to this is that this is certainly so. They are very soft if prepared properly and bream especially are very fond of them. There are times when bream will only touch a gozzer and will not be interested in anything else; this applies particularly on hard fished waters. Apart from this, the gozzer is a high quality bait, and if all the bait you use is of a good quality your confidence will be high and a confident angler is a successful angler. I prefer to spend my time preparing first class baits, which I regard as vitally important, rather than wasting time on ensuring that my tackle is always neat and tidy, which only impresses inexperienced anglers and does not help me to catch more fish!

Redworms. I must mention redworms, as these can be an excellent bait in summer, and can give you the added bonus catch of big perch or tench. I will not keep the worm for a long time, but I prefer to get

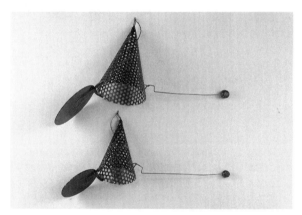

Bait droppers come in all shapes and sizes. The types shown at the top are Dickie's favourites.

Shoebox for breeding gozzers. Meat is simply placed on a small tray inside.

fresh worms for each trip. This may sound strange, but it is in line with my idea of always using only fresh bait, which I have mentioned before.

Bread. Crust cubes should be cut with a sharp knife, and can be fished on the bottom. I do little of this type of fishing now, but it can be very pleasant for a few hours' pleasure fishing on a summer evening, using a long piece of elastic on the pole in case of big fish.

Bread Punch. The good thing about bread punch fishing is that you can have a successful day's fishing for a low cost, which makes a change from the high cost of other baits. To prepare bread for the punch, I get a medium sliced loaf and cut off the crust. I then boil a kettle and hold the bread in the steam to dampen it slightly. I then roll the bread flat with a rolling pin, place it in a polythene bag and put it in the fridge. I normally do this two days before I am likely to need the bread as bait. As mentioned earlier a lot of people still prefer to roll the bread as shown, but another way of preparing your bread is to buy a fresh sliced loaf. A more dense loaf (less air holes) is best, and without rolling it, steam it over a kettle on the morning of the match and place in a polythene bag. For punch fishing now, there seem to be two different ways of ground baiting.

Preparing bread for use with bread punch.

1. Cutting off crusts.

2. Lightly dampening bread over a hot, steaming kettle.

3. Rolling bread.

4. The finished bait.

(a) A very coarse white crumb. To mix this correctly, I put a drop of water into the ground bait bowl (round bowls being best) and add groundbait. Fluff and shake it very dry. Also to the water I like to add a bit of my D. C. Roach Attractor. When this is a reasonably dry texture, I get a maggot sieve, and just sieve the groundbait through. Any lumps left on top of the sieve I throw away. This is then ready for use.

(b) The second method, which a lot of people seem to prefer, is to buy a sliced loaf and cut off the crust, then put it through a liquidiser. Afterwards put it into a polythene bag and put it in the fridge overnight—it is now ready for use. You know if you've got the bread right if with groundbaits and bait you are able to squeeze together in hand and throw it out, and it should float on the surface before it breaks slowly and sinks. Then you know it is just right for punch fishing.

Bloodworms and Jokers. Bloodworms are the bait which have caused more controversy than any other, except perhaps hemp in the past. The bloodworm is not, in fact, a worm, but is the larva of the midge. It is used very widely in the south of England, but has been banned at some venues in the northern part of the country. I feel I should make it clear at this point that I don't agree with bait bans. I go fishing to catch fish, not to find out what *does* catch them—and then ban it! One of the reasons given for the ban is that not everyone could afford to buy the large quantities of bait which are required; in my opinion, the solution to this problem is to go out and collect your own.

I honestly believe that most ponds contain bloodworm, and that anyone can obtain them if they put themselves out a bit. You will need chest waders and a scraper for bloodworm collecting. The scraper is attached to a pole and is home-made, with a stainless steel bottom. The blade should be about 12 inches long, one inch in depth, and one sixteenth of an inch thick. The bloodworms live just under the surface of the bottom mud with their 'heads' sticking out a bit into the water. The blade of the scraper is drawn along just under the surface of the mud. At the end of each stroke, with the blade flat, a quick movement is made with the wrist to turn the blade so that it is face up, or the bloodworm will fall off. It is then lifted straight up and the blade is banged onto a sieve, which floats in the water beside the collector. A net is attached to the underside of the sieve, and the bloodworm fall into this net. A fine mesh is required or the bloodworm will escape. When you reach home, add a little peat to the bloodworms, and then put them in the fridge at 40 or 45 degrees Fahrenheit; an essential item of equipment, that fridge, for the pole angler!

Jokers are 'mini-bloodworms', and are used solely as attractors. They are found in shallow flowing waters, often below sewage outfalls. The usual method of collection is to disturb the mud first with a stick, when the jokers float up and can be collected in a fine mesh net. Add peat, wrap them in newspaper, and put them in the fridge with the larger blood-worms.

Hemp. I prefer to cook my hemp the night before I am going to use it as an attractor. If I am going to fish with chrysoidine maggots I sometimes drop small crystals of chrysoidine* into the water when cooking the hemp. This colours the water orange and part of the pieces of hemp will also be dyed this colour, and this works well as a bait. Rhodamine can be used in the same way. I recommend using the largest size of hemp you can obtain, which is usually known as the Chilean variety. Cook the hemp slowly on gas no. 1 or 2 until the grains start to split, then stand it outside to cool. Different colour dyes are worth trying and the hemp should be taken to the waterside in a sealed polythene bag.

Groundbait. Many anglers seem to think that the purpose of groundbait is to feed the fish, but I use it mainly to carry the loose bait to the bottom. I think that the groundbait should form a 'smelly' cloud which will attract the fish, and will keep them in the area so that they will take the hookbaits. This is especially true in winter, when the fish eat less, so the groundbait should include only a small quantity of feed. Most proprietary groundbaits contain as much as 80% feed, which I think is too much—this is too filling for the fish. The French match anglers use mainly china clay or soil to form their cloud; 50% of their groundbait will be the clay or soil, and only 50% bait, such as bloodworm, which the clay or soil will help carry to the bottom. This is one of my reasons for making sure my bread groundbait is as fine as possible—so that it forms a good cloud.

Anyone who has the time and who is prepared to do tests, can find out for themselves the best way to use groundbait, but I will describe what I have found to be the best method, after long experience. Especially in the canals and rivers, I find it best to put some groundbait in the area, and to time how long it takes to get a bite. The float can be put up in up to a metre away from the cloud to see how well the cloud and the smell of the bait is working.

---

* There has been some publicity in the angling journals and in daily newspapers about the possibility that the use of chrysoidine dye may be connected with some forms of cancer. It now seems likely that this substance is dangerous and readers are advised not to use it under any circumstances. A substitute is now available from most good tackle shops.

Bloodworm—shown here with one penny piece to indicate size. Jokers are usually
about half this size and are generally used for feeding only.

When catching fish on top, I prefer to have the groundbait very
wet. Bob Nudd, who I have mentioned before, is very good at catching
fish from the top four feet of water but he mixes his groundbait much
dryer. He takes a caster sieve with him, and sieves his groundbait to
get rid of any lumps. There can then be no big pieces to fill the fish
up quickly—only cloud to attract.

The French and Belgians, when fishing on top, often use powdered
ground cork, which makes a good cloud when mixed in with breadcrumbs,
as it doesn't hold together on its own.

It undoubtedly helps to have an attractive groundbait, and there
are many additives which will help to improve the attractiveness of the
groundbait. Their efficiency can be tested by doing some experiments
with fish in tanks, which the French often do. Catch some fish, put them
into a tank, and drop different types of groundbait into a corner of the
tank, keeping records of the reactions of the fish to each type. A lot
can be learned in this way, but if you are unable to do this sort of experiment, then you will only be able to find out which additives are best
by trial and error in actual fishing situations.

Some of the additives I have tried are:

Vanilla, which is good for bream, as they seem to like sweet flavours.

Dickie is seen here with his joker net, which he uses to scrape along the bottom of the stream gathering up the jokers, sediment and general debris. The net is then held by the top and agitated in the stream until the contents are reasonably clean. It is then transferred to a bucket and taken home and put into the joker bag.

Dickie's joker bag, which he uses to submerge in a tank of water allowing the jokers to make their way out leaving the sediment behind in the bag.

A well-used groundbait mixing bowl.

Maple, also good for bream.

Pineapple, another good additive for bream groundbaits.

Crushed hemp, which is a very well known groundbait additive for roach.

Fenugreek, also very good for roach.

Camaline, used a lot by the French as a roach attractor.

Cocoa, another good attractor for roach.

Maize, fine maize, well sieved and mixed with groundbait, is very good.

Ground Rice, makes a good cloud groundbait.

Sunflower Seed, in powder form often works well for surface feeding roach.

Sweet Biscuits, another good additive for bream.

Ground coconut shell, a friend in Ireland told me about the use of this which they have found to be very good for bream; you use only about 10% in your groundbait mix.

Pumpkinseed Meal, works well as a good small fish attractor.

Hemp Water, when fishing bloodworm in winter I prefer to overcook my hemp and take the 'hemp water' to the match in a flask and mix it with the groundbait—a good tip.

Concentrated Sweetener. Recently I have been using a liquid sweetener and adding it to my groundbait at a rate of one teaspoon per ten ounce mix. I got the idea from Kevin Maddocks who uses it with great success for carp and he tells me that liquid Hermesetas is as good

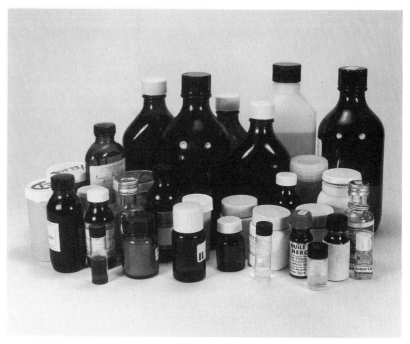

The vast selection of flavours and colours available gives the pole angler the opportunity to create 'new' baits which can be an advantage on hard fished waters.

as any other concentrated sweetener for cyprinids. At one stage I told Kevin I had run out and also that I had won nothing for two weeks. After obtaining a new bottle from Kevin I went on to win the next two matches using the sweetener.

Other flavours are: caramel, cinnamon, spearmint, cream, molasses, dried blood, trout pellets, crushed prawns, fructose (fruit sugar), liver extract, Oxo cubes and soy bean oil.

Once you find the flavours that seem to work well for you, you will have confidence in them, and this confidence is important in angling.

Groundbait

In the last five years the market in England for the continental type groundbait has increased tremendously. There is no one reason for this but rather a combination of a few. Probably the most influential factor was availability of top quality joker especially in the south of England.

This led to anglers being able to fish with bloodworm and joker properly. However the next thing needed was a decent groundbait to use. Marcel Van Den Eynde provided this groundbait. Although he has been manufacturing groundbait for over 20 years it only reached our shops five years ago. It is a recognised fact that his groundbaits are the best in the world. Previously, English anglers had had to make do with either brown or white crumb which does not offer the different textures needed, or substandard, mainly French, products which were no good for the English market.

There had always been some mystique attached to continental groundbaits; all the different ingredients and aromas had us all confused. However, now I have learnt that the only variation needed is texture. To explain this further: what I require is a number of different textures for a number of different situations. I will describe these and tell you what groundbait recipe I would use for each. First of all I will give you a brief rundown of the different groundbaits I use.

Years ago even the people lucky enough to be able to get jokers and bloodworm in reasonable quantities could never seem to get 'filling it in' to work as they do on the Continent. I must admit that I thought that fish in England must be different and would not put up with loads of groundbait being thrown at them. Now we know how wrong we were; we just did not use the right groundbait. What we needed was groundbait with the right qualities, ie., texture and binding.

Secret

This really is a base mix, which is a sticky, heavy groundbait. The fact that it is the biggest selling groundbait in Europe is no surprise. Secret is a proven bream attractor but its binding qualities are what interest me. For rivers I use one part Secret, one part Vijver and a handful of Grey Leem to get my bait to the bottom quickly. When there is extra flow on or in a naturally fast river I would add half a bag of cod fat to this mix to help bind it. Coolart has the advantage of being an excellent binder but it also helps break your mix up once it has hit the bottom.

Special

This is a superfine cloud groundbait. As with all Marcel's baits the ingredients are top secret but this has a rather sweet smell and creates a fantastic cloud. When fishing on the drop on canals and lakes for small fish with any hookbait I use Special on its own, mixed on the dry side so it just holds together.

One tip I learnt from Marcel is to add Special to other mixes. Its clouding qualities help it attract fish into your peg immediately. On canals when I am using jokers as feed and I intend putting an opening barrage of feed in to create a bed of feed on the bottom, I use a bag of Secret mixed with a bag of Special and then of course some Grey Leem to hold the two very different textures together.

Vijver

Vijver is probably the best roach groundbait I have ever used. The name Vijver is Flemish for lake and that is where this groundbait is most effective. As far as texture goes it is somewhere between Secret and Special. It is easy to mix up and squeezes nicely when loose offerings are added. Although this mix is primarily designed for lakes I have experimented with Vijver on rivers by mixing it with cod fat and Grey Leem to help it get to the bottom quickly.

Expo

Expo is a red groundbait similar in texture to Secret. This is the groundbait for tench and carp; don't ask me why, but it is. I have asked Marcel what it is in Expo that carp and tench like but all he does is smile at me. The funny thing is that a couple of years ago we had a 'rodent' problem in our warehouse and do you know that out of all the different groundbait ingredients etc, that were on offer, the only groundbait that was eaten was Expo!

Whenever I go on a venue in the summer where there is a chance of tench or carp I also throw a couple of bags of Expo in the bait bag. It is easy to mix up and has a fine sweet smell. My partner Richard Borley first discovered its qualities for carp fishing on a Match of the Year semi-final at Arrow Valley lakes. He practised during the week on the lake and caught carp, loads of them. The only reason he used Expo was that it was the only one he had in his bag. Anyway on the match he used four bags of Expo in conjunction with the pole and bloodworm to come second with 17lb of carp up to 7lb. The funny thing is that the final was on a lake in Ireland and Richard used Expo again and won the Matchman of the Year title, not with carp but with perch!

The whole range of Marcel Van Den Eynde's groundbaits consists of ten different mixes, all of which are worth using. Some of them are more suited to rod and line or feeder tactics, but they are all worth a try. The beauty is that you can mix any number of them together; experiment for yourself, you may come up with a winner. Just to give you a guide I will set them out in binding quality: Kanal, Secret, Expo, World Champion, Beet, Kastaar, Natuur, Vijver, Super Cup, Special.

Mixing

Although Marcel has produced these groundbaits so that mixing them is easy, to get the right results follow these little tips to get it right all of the time.

First of all use a round groundbait bowl so that no groundbait gets caught in any corners and spoils the texture of the mix. If you intend mixing two of the baits together mix them thoroughly before adding water. Once this is done, add water gradually, not all at once but just a bit at a time. I use a sponge and squeeze it over the bowl as I mix the groundbait with my fingers. Once you have got the mix about right put it aside for ten minutes and you will probably find that it needs a touch more water; again just add it gradually. You will know when the mix is right by squeezing it and if it holds together and you can still crumble it back to near its normal condition by rubbing it between your fingers, you've cracked it.

Most anglers will be satisfied at this stage but I do like to take it a bit further. I mix my groundbait the night before a match and then when it is done I put it on top of a maggot sieve and rub it through. This has the effect of taking out the lumps. Next job is to put it in a polythene bag and tie the top up to keep the moisture in.

Coolart

Coolart is another one of Marcel's products; it is simply a binder. Although it is very sticky it can be added to any mix to get it to the bottom quickly and as I have said before it has the added advantage of breaking up quickly.

Leem

Leem comes in three different varieties. Firstly, Damp Leem which is the same colour as the other two, grey and brown, but it has the moisture left in so it is a lot heavier. I use Damp Leem to add weight to my groundbait when fishing deep water, usually when joker is the feed. It can be used on its own without groundbait when you want to feed joker alone. The weight of the Damp Leem together with the moisture mean that you can add it to the joker and still squeeze balls together just as you can with ordinary groundbait.

Damp Leem is a great medium for keeping jokers in. I have come home from a match and put a pint of jokers in a handful of Damp Leem and they have still been alive a week later.

Grey Leem

This was a brilliant discovery made by Richard Borley. So many people have tried to find out what it is or where it comes from but no-one has and I can assure you that no-one ever will. Grey Leem has two different qualities. They come from its very dry nature which soaks up moisture very quickly. On a lot of canals nowadays it has become fashionable to feed jokers neat. Now as many of you will know it is impossible to throw neat jokers any distance. If you sprinkle two teaspoons of Grey Leem to half a pink of jokers and mix it in you will be able to throw it as far as you like.

In the 1988 World Championships the victorious England team all used Grey Leem to feed neat jokers both on a pole and waggler line. Needless to say none of the other teams had Grey Leem and they could not feed neat jokers at distance.

The other use for Grey Leem is to bind groundbait together. It is not difficult but I will explain. Mix your groundbait as normal. When it is ready put your jokers on top of the groundbait and then sprinkle a little Grey Leem on to the jokers and mix them in, just like making a cake. Just keep adding a little Grey Leem at a time until when you squeeze a ball it stays together and shows no signs of falling apart. If you are on deep or fast flowing water and you want to put a lot of loose feed in your groundbait, jokers or maggots, mix in the Grey Leem as I have described, squeeze the balls you require and then wet your hands and give each ball a coating of water, sort of glaze them. This has the effect of keeping them together as they hit the surface.

You may find that Grey Leem is difficult to use and until you get a feel for how much to use you may have problems. However, here are two little tips if you get stuck. If your mix is too wet add more Grey Leem, if it is too dry a lot of anglers are using a spray, as used for spraying indoor plants, to add very small amounts of water evenly to the mix.

Magic. This works very well, and it sinks quickly, so it is best for deep water. It is good for roach, skimmers and gudgeon. This groundbait holds plenty of feed and is a good all-round groundbait for deepish water.

I usually feed these groundbaits in small pieces about the size of a fingernail and put the float accurately into the centre of the cloud caused by the groundbait. Bites are often instant, especially with the last two groundbaits mentioned.

Before I try to give the reader some idea of how I feed with these groundbaits, I must emphasise once more that it is most important NOT to put too much feed in the groundbait, especially when using the heavier feeds which you want to get to the bottom quickly. Putting in too much

Dickie prefers to feed whilst holding the pole, keeping the pole tip close to the water and using it as a marker for the groundbait.

feed or not putting it in at the right time, can easily frighten the fish away instead of keeping them in the swim.

There are no set rules on how to feed; only experience will show the best way, but some guidelines may help.

I will start with the methods I use for feeding in deeper water where the object is to get the feed down onto the bottom as quickly as possible. I use golf ball sized pieces to start with and I don't feed any more until I start to catch. If I feel that the fish are easing off in their feeding, then I will put another ball in, but this time it will only be about half the size of a golf ball. Try to work out how the fish are reacting to the way you are feeding and fishing, and this will tell you if, and when, to put more feed in. Since the amounts and frequency required vary from day to day, and from venue to venue, only experience and experimentation will enable you to get it right.

Feeding the shallow swims on canals and still waters is much easier, although I don't feed on canals when lock gates are opening and shutting. I put nothing in at the start, and feed while I am fishing with small balls of very wet, sloppy groundbait, each about the size of a 1p piece. I find the best way to get the maggots etc., into the bait is to take a

Elastics come in various strengths.

pinch of the maggots from the bait box, drop it onto the groundbait, pinch the bait round it, and then flick it out.

I feed every cast, with four or five bits of bait in the groundbait each time. This keeps a cloud in the swim all the time, with only a small amount of feed. You must be very accurate when putting the groundbait in. Don't spread it out, but try to keep it in an area of about 18 inches square.

Red Dye. I have been using a lot of red dye as mentioned before, and now have dyes in the shops with my name on, and have supplied anglers of the calibre of Wayne Swiscoe and Tom Pickering, who are always asking me for more; it must be good if anglers of this class like it!

There are three colours available—blood red, yellow and bronze. the red is the most popular, and scientific experiments have shown that fish can see colours on the red side of the spectrum best, which explains why these dyes have done so well.

These dyes are non-toxic and research chemist Mike Kelly says you could drink them without any ill effect, so it might be well worth trying

Dickie admires the pole extension with a built-in hand warmer made by Don Neish. Dickie is now using longer poles up to 14 metres in length and has recently purchased a 'Long John' pole of 12.1 metres with extension top joint to 13 metres.

Dickie unhooks a nice chub.

these dyes for a change—I am a great believer in trying something different, as I have said elsewhere in the book.

That is all I wish to say about baits and groundbaiting at present, although I will offer some more advice when I suggest ways of using each float in the following chapter.

Don't forget — discarded line kills birds and other wild animals

Floats and Float Set-ups

There are so many different kinds of floats that I think that float buying tends to catch more anglers than it does fish. I intend to illustrate eighteen different types of floats and the set-ups to be used with them and will also try to explain, as best I can, what each rig is meant to do. Before I do this, however, I want to make a couple of general points in relation to floats.

I consider that the best colour for the tops of floats is normally yellow, white or red. In open water where there are no shadows I think that black is best. I always carry with me a small bottle of Tipp-Ex, which is a white typewriter eraser and which can be brushed onto the float should a lighter colour be required. Tipp-Ex dries almost immediately, so this is a very quick way of changing the float colours when needed.

When float fishing in shallow water, I don't like to have the part of the float that is underneath the water black in colour, although most floats, when bought, are painted black at the bottom. I am sure that grey, white or blue are less conspicuous colours. If you look at the under-sides of all birds which eat fish you will find that they are white or blue underneath, so these colours must be the best camouflage, as the fish can obviously see them less easily—which is a very good reason for having your float one of these colours, at least for the part that is under the water.

Before listing floats and their shotting patterns etc., I think the reader will find the comparison table on page 56, of lead sizes very useful.

I will now list each float I use, what I use it for, and the shotting patterns I recommend. Remember that these may well need altering at times—nothing can be definite in angling, so these should only be used as a rough guide:

1 and 4. These floats are very similar. I like to use them in fairly deep water which is either still or slow moving. Both floats are fixed top and bottom, and are shotted as shown in the diagrams. I like to use these floats to register bites on the drop, and you can see by their shape that they are suitable for this.

When using these floats, I like to loose feed whenever possible and

COMPARISON TABLE OF LEAD* SIZES
WITH WEIGHTS IN GRAMS
Kindly supplied by Don Neish of Don's of Edmonton

Round Split Shot		Olivette Paquita		Olivette Torpille		Olivette Comte-Stix		Precision Styl Leads		Mouse Dropping		Celery Shot	
size	gram	size	gram	size	gram	size	gram	size	gram	size	gram	size	gram
LG	4.72												
SG	3.54												
		12	3.00										
SPSG	2.57	11	2.45	11	2.50								
		10	2.10	10	2.00								
SSG	1.89	9	1.85										
		8	1.56	9	1.50								
		7	1.36							5x20	1.24		
		6	1.16	8	1.20								
		5a	.92	7	1.00					4x17	.95		
AAA	.81	5	.82	6	.80								
		4a	.78			8	.78						
		4	.67			7	.65			3x12	.67	1	.6
				5	.60								
		3a	.57			6	.55						
				4	.50								
		3	.44			5	.45						
BB	.40	2a	.40	3	.40								
		2	.37			4	.33			2½x10	.36	2	.3
		1a	.31	2	.30								
1	.28					3	.28						
		1	.25			2	.24	20	.258				
3	.20	0a	.20	1	.20	1	.20			2¼x9	.21		
4	.17	0	.17			1	.18	18	.170	2x7	.17	3	.17
5	.13	2/0	.13	0	.13			16	.130			4	.13
6	.105	3/0	.105					15	.103	1¾x6	.10		
7	.083	4/0	.081					14	.084	1½x5	.08	5	.08
8	.063							13	.070				
9	.049							12	.052				
								11	.040				
10	.034							10	.031				
11	.026												
								9	.022				
12	.020												
								8	.015				
13	.012												
								7	.010				

1 ounce = 28.3495 grams   1 gram = 0.035274 ounces

*Styl lead weights can still be used but lead is now illegal in many weights, and Olivettes are now usually made of tungsten. This table was compiled for lead weights but as the weights in the new materials are so similar it is still valid.

Choosing your weights according to their gram weight will allow a wider range of shotting arrangements and quick conversion from one type of weight to another.

Whereas the older style of markings (e.g. 5BB) offered limited scope the same float marked 2.00 grams may be shotted in countless ways to suit varying conditions.

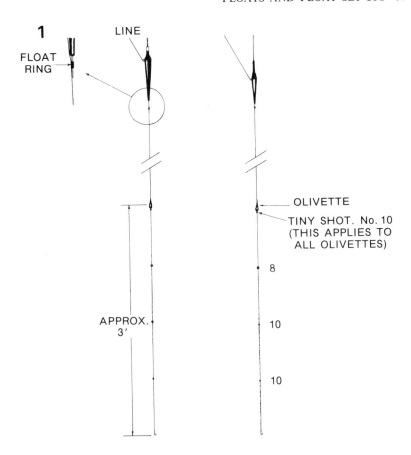

if I am using groundbait I like it to be of the slow sinking type, which forms a cloud as it goes down. You can fish these floats either with the bait on the bottom, or just off it, as they are very sensitive floats. The floats fish well with maggots, pinkies, bloodworms or almost any other type of bait, and in my opinion are the sort of floats which every pole angler should have in his box.

If I am catching 'on the drop' (when the fish takes the bait whilst it is sinking) when fishing with these floats, I like to have some sample hook maggots which float, as these counter-balance the weight of the hook which makes the bait sink more naturally and look more like a free offering.

2 and 3. Although these two floats are slighly different in shape,

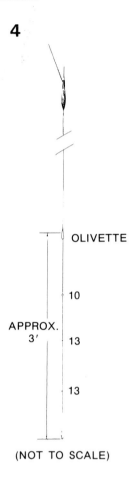

they both do roughly the same job. I like to use these in moving waters at any depth, but the deeper the water, the larger the float, of course. They are good for fishing with hemp and casters, although they can be used with other baits such as maggots, especially during the summer months. I overshot these floats and edge them down along the swim on a very short line when weather conditions are poor. If conditions are in your favour, a longer length of line can be used, as long as you make sure at all times that you have perfect control.

As you will see from the diagrams the shotting patterns are the same, but can be varied slightly according to the behaviour of the fish.

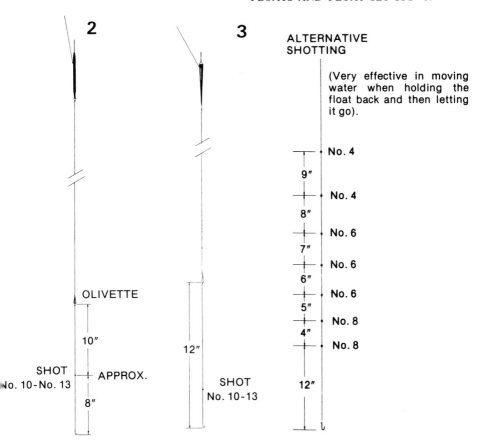

During the summer months, I feed when using these floats by putting in a couple of bait dropper-fulls of hemp or caster on the bottom, so that I know exactly where the bait is, and that it is where I want it. After this, I feed every cast. I have a mixture of two-thirds casters, one-third hemp, in the same bowl. I add some water, then feed with a pinch of the mix, which will contain perhaps eight casters to four pieces of hemp per pinch, just behind the float on each cast. The bait is therefore going in about every 30 seconds. So that I miss few bites, I use a size 18 hook for this type of fishing, and I also like to use some floating casters from time to time, as hook baits which have not been in water, to make the bait look more natural, as previously described. These floats have a harder shell which helps to prevent the size 18 hook from coming

out of the bait. Fishing this method, you will find that you do pick up some good quality roach and dace at times.

5. This may well be a funny-looking float, but I have found it to be a very good one when I want to get the bait down quickly. With this one I like to use bloodworm, with a heavy groundbait as mentioned earlier to get the bait down quickly, which it will do if shotted as in the diagram, or in a similar way.

This is a good set-up for use in deepish water, which is either still or has only a slight flow. I have had many good catches of skimmer bream in this way.

If you are using this float, as I have already said, it means that you will be using a heavy groundbait to get the bait to the bottom quickly. You can either use china clay or soil, but if you choose to use soil I consider it important to use the actual soil from the bank of the water you are fishing, rather than to take the soil with you. Have a sieve with you and take the soil from as close to the water as possible, so that it will be the same colour as that which the fish are used to. Using a soil even very slightly different in colour may put the fish off. Remember that the soil is only a vehicle for getting the bloodworm to the bottom, so that you can keep the amount of feed to a minimum to prevent the fish from being filled up too quickly with free offerings.

When fishing deep water I like to put my feed in at the beginning, as the Continentals do, and only add to the feed when I think that the fish have taken most of the bait on the bottom and are looking for more.

If bream or other bigger fish are the quarry it pays to fish three or four bloodworm on the hook, and this works very well for bream. With this number of bloodworm, it is best to use a size 20 hook, and I prefer the Mustad 5715 or 5713; the 5715 (barbless) is for swinging to hand and the 5713 (barbed) for taking apart.

6. This is a bit of a specialist float, which I use solely for fishing bloodworm. As you can see, it has a very long antenna because it is used for lifting and dropping the bait all the time. Used in various depths of still or slow moving water, the float is overshotted so that the antenna sinks slowly, then is lifted again to cause the bloodworm to move up and down near the bottom, just as the jokers do naturally.

7. This float started to become popular in 1979, the year the Germans won the World Championship, because it is very similar to the float they used then. It is very good for fishing with long lines when swinging to hand, and for use in fast and turbulent waters. It gets the bait to the bottom very quickly and holds its position well in fast water. It can be used with different baits and is another type of float every pole angler should have available. Although the body shapes can vary, they are all used for the same job. With maggots and casters, use with a bait dropper to get the bait in the right place on the bottom. Use of this float is the only way in which you can guarantee to fish where the feed is, in fast and turbulent water.

8. This type of float is normally home-made, and is simple both to make and to use. Shotted as in the diagram, this float is for still water and canals of up to 5 to 6ft in depth.

The float is fished well over depth, up to four feet, in fact, with normally a couple of number 10 shot lying on the bottom. Bites are usually 'sail-aways'. This is a light float so it should be fished without too long a line between the pole and the float, when it seems to work exceptionally well for caster fishing for roach. I like to have it shotted so that the top of the float only just projects from the water.

9 and 10. These floats are both for fishing in the top 3–4 feet of the water for small fish such as bleak, small roach and dace, and the

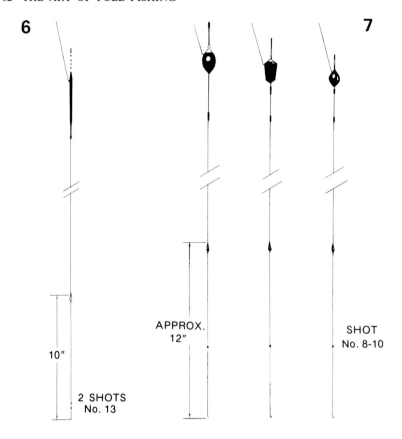

6

7

10"

2 SHOTS
No. 13

APPROX.
12"

SHOT
No. 8-10

swing-to-hand method is used. No. 9 is a small piece of peacock quill, fished double rubber. I leave it white in colour apart from the top, which is painted black or red. I find this excellent for use in a similar way to a stick float, easing the bait along in coloured water, and holding the float back so that the bait lifts up a little in the water; you usually catch when holding back. It is very good in running water, whereas no. 10, which is shotted in the same way, I find most effective in still water. Using no. 10 I have caught as many as 28 lb of small carp in a five hour match in the top three feet of the water. These floats are much favoured by the Italians for speed fishing, as both are only one inch long.

As you will be fishing shallow water with these floats, the only way to keep fish constantly interested is to keep the bait falling through your

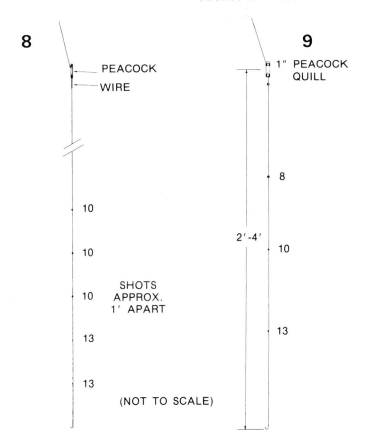

swim all the time, so I recommend using a bait apron, and feeding about 12 maggots at least every 30 seconds. In this way you will be sure to keep the fish constantly attracted to the baited area.

Of course, if bites do cease, it is always worth trying deeper, because the constant feeding may well have attracted fish to feed deeper in the water, and you may well pick up quality fish in this way. If you think you may want to do this, it is worth having a spare pole and set-up ready to try the deeper water, such as nos 1 or 2.

11. Another specialist float, which might be described as more of a casting weight, or controller, than a float. With this I use a very soft telescopic pole, with the line only two or three inches shorter than the

pole length. The hook length should be from 12oz to 1lb BS, and can be anything from a foot to three feet long. Use a very fine wire size 20 hook to keep the weight down, as you are going to use this float for fishing the bait on the surface. The hook is attached to the main line with 'invisible' thread of 2lb BS nylon, of a type that 'crinkles', or coils, very easily. Once you have tied on the hook, run a fingernail along the last 8–9 inches of the 2lb line near the hook length to make this part of the line lie in coils on the surface. The coils will be greased to make them float. There will be 18 inches to two feet of line below the float plus the hook length. Watch the coil as it floats on the surface of the water, and when it starts to 'unwind', you have a bite. Don't strike too hard, but pull the hook into the fish.

Dickie's tackle box—not the neatest in the game but one of the most effective.

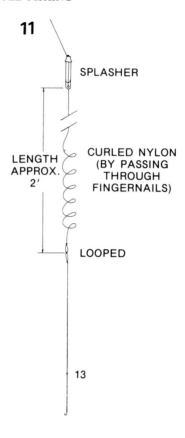

With this surface rig, no shot will be used, and the hook length is best kept to about 12 inches, if the fish are taking at the surface. If they start to take below the surface, lengthen the hook line and add a no. 13 shot to make the bait sink slowly. If the fish are still further down, perhaps a foot deep, use three no. 13's, well spaced out.

This is a good method for surface feeding bleak, and is very effective for rudd in the same way, although the tackle should be stepped up a bit for rudd. It is best to feed three different areas with this type of fishing, moving the bait from one to the other, and feeding little and often, so that fish are not frightened out of the baited areas. A few years back I had 208 fish in an hour with this method, while the French have caught up to 250 fish an hour, and the Italians over 300 an hour in this way. It is a good idea to put a bit of Mystic paste over the shank

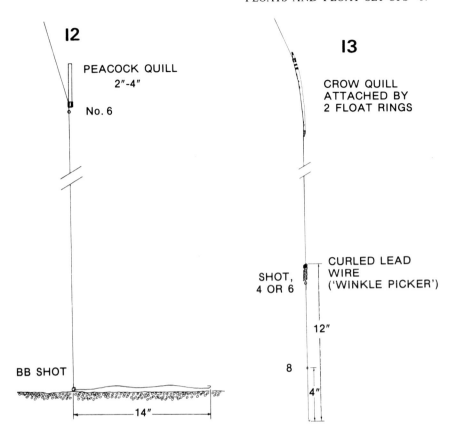

12

PEACOCK QUILL
2"-4"

No. 6

BB SHOT

|← 14" →|

13

CROW QUILL
ATTACHED BY
2 FLOAT RINGS

SHOT,
4 OR 6

CURLED LEAD
WIRE
('WINKLE PICKER')

12"

8

4"

of the hook, or to use an eyed hook, to prevent the maggot from being blown up the line on each bite.

12. A very simple float, this one, a piece of peacock quill about four inches long which you can cut up yourself. This is the lift method float, a method I was taught in the King's Arms and Eastern Enfield clubs. This works well for gravel pit tench and roach, especially for bread in summer. The bait lies on the bottom, and there is one shot just touching bottom. As the fish takes the bait, the shot is lifted, and the float lies flat, or simply runs away.

I have enjoyed many happy hours fishing with this float and method, and have found it very effective using either crust or bread for tench. You can go up to size 8 or 10 hooks when using crust, and once you have put a little brown crumb on the bottom, all you have to do is sit and wait.

13. The 'old Jim Crow', or crow quill, is a very effective float when attached by double rubbers as shown, or reversed and attached by the bottom end only for canals. I will tell you how I use this one, which was first used on the Thames, and still is, for that matter. It is very good when the river is up and coloured, and 'pushing through'; I used it recently on a flooded River Ouse in a Winter League match, and had a very good result.

Fish downstream and use a weight which is made from coiled lead wire. This is put round a matchstick, and when it is wound round the line, the matchstick is removed. The lead ledger is stopped by a BB shot about 12 inches from the hook, as in the diagram. The float is held back and a bite pulls the line through the coiled lead wire in the same way as it does when ledgering. Bites on this float either tilt it up, or it slides away.

In these conditions, why not ledger with a rod and reel, I might be asked? In fact the method I have described here, using the pole, is better, because the line comes down in a straight line from the end of the pole, with far less line in the water than when using a rod and reel. The float is more easily controlled, while there is much less line in the water to pick up rubbish or to be affected by drag in the strong current. During the winter it helps to keep the bait still, which is often what the fish want. I recommend every pole angler to carry this float.

A good bait to use with this float in coloured water is yellow maggots, and the only way to get them where you want them in these conditions is to use a maggot dropper. Put the groundbait in about 2ft behind the float, and the flow will take the maggots down. The best way to do this is to have a spare pole set up with a maggot dropper attached ready, and with a 4lb line. If you put the dropper on your normal tackle, you might well lose it on the light line.

14 and 15. These two floats are basically the same, the only difference being that no. 15 is a lot bigger, so that it can be used in the deeper water of from five to nine feet. No. 14 I prefer to use in canals or very shallow lakes. Both floats are attached by the bottom end only.

When fishing this way on very fragile pole tackle I do recommend placing a piece of very fine rubber tubing, or a sleeve, on the line, and pinching the shot on this. This gives you the advantage of being able to alter the float depth very easily, and also the line cannot be damaged in any way. Shotting patterns as in the diagram.

When fishing with this float, especially on canals, I am usually after gudgeon, small roach, small bream, or perch, etc. I start by plumbing the depth very carefully, so that I know exactly what the bottom is like, as I am going to fish my bait no more than $\frac{1}{4}$ or $\frac{1}{2}$ an inch from the bottom. When I have discovered the exact depth, I mark it on the pole,

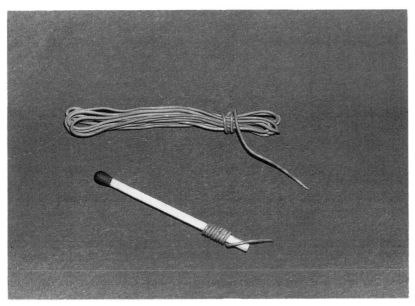

Lead wire wrapped around matchstick, for overshotting purposes as described in text.

so that if I get broken, or lose a hook length, I do not have to test the depth again, and perhaps frighten the fish with the plummet by doing so. As mentioned when writing about float no. 14, this is one of the times when I require a cloud groundbait, and a fine wire hook. This float registers bites on the drop as well, and if weather conditions allow I will swing to hand when using this float, although in bad conditions I may have to dismantle.

This method and float is very good for bloodworm fishing, and recently I have found that by feeding with jokers in the groundbait, instead of bloodworms, I have had some very good results in matches. Most people were using bloodworms rather than jokers, and my use of the jokers—something different again—gave me the edge over others, or so I believe.

Now to the bigger float, no. 15. Many anglers might say that a float attached by the bottom end should not be used in deep water, but I have found this float very effective at Cooks Ferry and other canal-like parts of the River Lea, and I will tell you why. I have often had great success while others were failing because my float was attached to the line by the bottom end only, and I fished it by putting the tip of the pole just under the water. The float then moved slowly downstream,

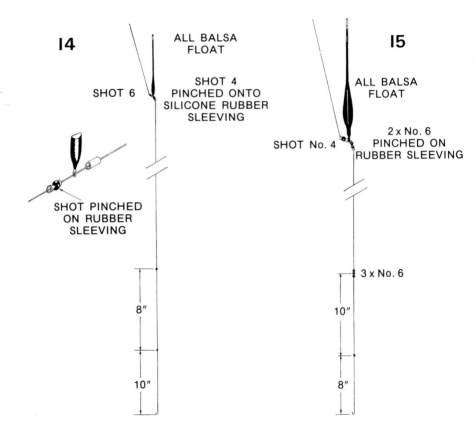

especially when the wind is blowing in the opposite direction to the flow because there was no line out of the water to catch the wind. Other anglers, with their floats attached top and bottom in the more conventional way for waters of this kind, found that their floats were stationary, or were even being blown upstream, and they did not get the bites. A bait moving in this way would not seem natural to the fish, although they would take baits which were moving downstream in the way which they would expect.

This large float is very good in deeper water when using maggots and casters for better fish, and I have done very well with it on the Lea using casters, and putting them in with a bait dropper.

16 and 17. These are the floats I use in Ireland, and I have put them in because so many people are now going to Ireland for fishing

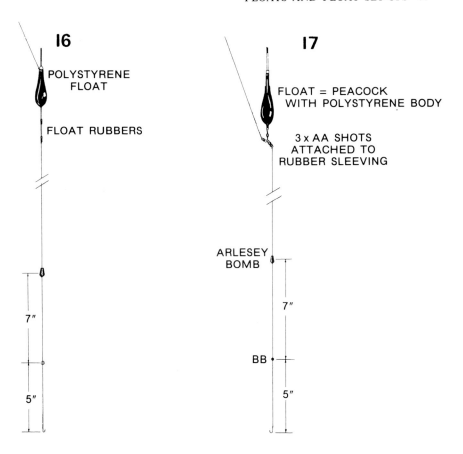

holidays. This is hardly surprising, as the fishing there must be rated the best in the world for this type of fishing. I have never seen any sign of any trouble, and have found the people to be very friendly.

Large amounts of groundbait are required for Irish fishing. To fish a five-hour match on the River Bann at Portadown, for example, I would take a gallon each of maggots and casters, and 25lb of groundbait.

Set the tackle up as shown in the diagram, normally using either 2.6 or 3.2lb breaking strain line for the hook lengths, tied to 4lb main line. As the floats are heavy to get the bait down, I always swing to hand. The line is attached to the tip of the pole as shown. When I get to the venue I start by putting in about 12 large balls of groundbait containing as much casters and hemp as possible. I might use as much as four pints of hemp in this way. I use groundbait dyed red with a food dye, while most people are using brown. Barbless hooks are best, and during a match I lift out everything of less than 1lb in weight. After the initial feeding, I put a lightly squeezed ball of groundbait in at every cast. Here I am after big catches, so I find it essential to make sure that all my tackle is laid out tidily around me, where I can reach it easily. You are fishing quickly to get these big weights so you may even wish to take the extreme measure of covering your hand with superglue, so that the hook point doesn't catch on the skin when you swing the fish in. To do this, hold the hand out with fingers spread, put on the glue, and leave it for a bit less than half a minute to dry; if you curl up the fingers before the glue sets they will stick together, so obviously care must be taken otherwise you could need the assistance of a surgeon!

From the diagrams you will see that an Arlesey bomb is used instead of shot, because it causes fewer tangles. The dropping shot will be a BB so that bites register clearly. Both the floats have large inserts and both are attached either double rubber, or by the bottom end only. A good idea with float no. 17, is to fix a swivel at the bottom of the float. This will then not be rigid, and will 'collapse' when a fish is hooked and you will get them every time. When trying for these big weights, it is important to miss as few fish as possible, or you are wasting time.

Red maggots fish well in Ireland, and I have found this to be one of the best baits. I usually use 2–3 maggots, and catch up to six fish on each lot of bait. You do not have to be really fast to get big weights in Ireland, but you must miss fewer fish; each time you come out without a fish is wasted time.

A float attached by the bottom end only is often best in Ireland, fished in the same way as I described in the previous section for fishing on the River Lea. If the float is attached at both ends it may well be held back too much.

A final point on fishing in Ireland is that it is always advisable to have a few runs through with the float before starting to put in the initial feed. This is to make sure that there is no rubbish or irregularities on the bottom, as you don't want to waste the bait in an unsuitable area.

18. This is a small float used for hemp fishing when the fish are in the top two to three feet of the water. A large amount of feed is used, and the float is weighted with 'celery' weights because you get fewer false bites with these weights than you would if you were using shot. You will need to feed at each cast with 30 or so grains of hemp every 30 seconds. Use the 39853 pattern hook, which is a very strong one, in size 14. You will need a hook of this kind as the method is to draw the float back towards you, and the fish take the hemp while it is moving, and hook themselves.

19. This is the grass float, which I like to use on shallow water

18

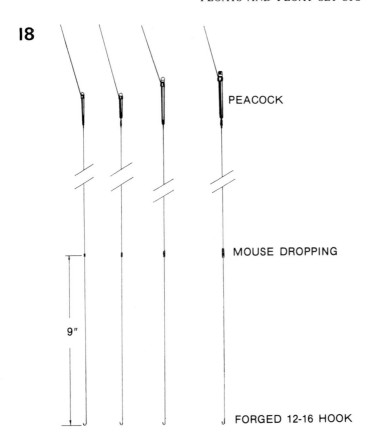

PEACOCK

MOUSE DROPPING

9"

FORGED 12-16 HOOK

especially on canals. It is the most sensitive float I have used, and I was shown this one by two other members of the England team, Dave Roper and Dave Brogden. To give some idea of how useful this float is, I should like to point out that in my last eleven matches I have had seven placings in the top three, and three wins using this float.

Catching fish on the drop is easy with this type of float, as they show every movement. They are ideal for use in shallow water in either canals or lakes, and they work to perfection in ideal summer conditions— when the weather is good and there is little wind.

Small baits such as bloodworm, pinkies and squats are used when catching small fish, especially on the drop. Many people use size 10 hooks with these floats, and with shots all down the line. I don't agree with

Tipp-Ex can be useful when a quick change of colour is required.

fishing in this way, as you miss many bites, so I prefer to use 6's and 8's. Fish will follow the bait down, and you will miss few bites. The best shotting pattern is as shown in the diagram.

I will now tell you how to go about making these floats, as they cannot be bought. Collect the grasses from a meadow where the grass is going brown in the autumn, and keep in a warm place to dry off for about six weeks. Cut the grass into the required lengths, from seven inches long to five inches, and cover the grass with the sealer used for rods to waterproof it. Then paint the tops red or black. Seal the top with Araldite and whip and glue an eye onto the bottom of each float. You can make the floats parallel or they can have an insert at the top. They are cheap to make, and the more you see them the more you will understand them. These grass floats will play a big part in my future fishing, and I believe that every pole angler should have one.

20. This little float is used for close-in fishing and is attached by double rubber. I use these a lot on canals for close-in gudgeon fishing. This float is based on an Italian type used a lot in summer conditions in Italy and also by Bob Nudd of Essex County. A small Olivette is placed on the line about eight inches from the hook with one very small

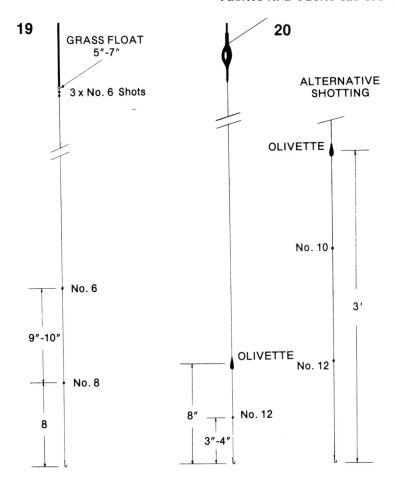

shot three inches from the hook; small bleak and roach will also be caught when using this float.

    21. This Ignesti is one of the few new floats that I'm going to mention but it is one that really works well. What I like about this float is the nice long stem, which makes it very stable, at the same time as being very sensitive. In the smaller sizes I found it exceptionally good for canals and shallow lakes. It can either be shortened as shown with Styl leads or an Olivette. I like to use the float version in conjunction with a bread punch on canals. I find the long stem makes it stable and I don't need a lot of weight down. It is very good too, in windy conditions which

21

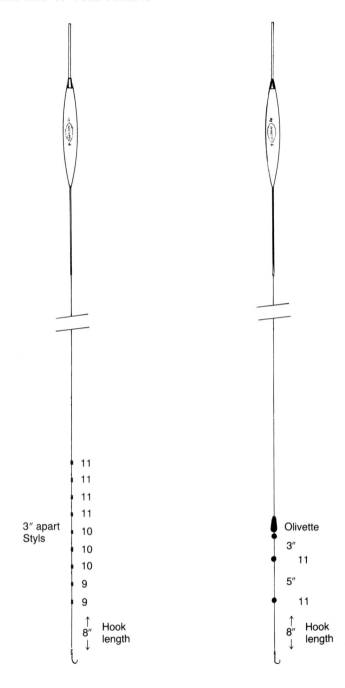

3″ apart
Styls

11
11
11
11
10
10
10
9
9

↑
8″
↓
Hook
length

Olivette

3″
11

5″
11

↑
8″
↓
Hook
length

is another advantage with this particular float. It also works very well for bloodworm fishing. It is very easy to work, to lift and drop, and see every movement on the float. I use an Olivette pattern as well when I need to get the bait down to the bottom—feeding fish quicker.

In deeper water I also use this float a lot, of course, in a slightly bigger size from 4×16 to 1 gm depending on depth and weather conditions. I've found it exceptionally good for laying on over-depth with caster, in fact for any still or slow moving water. I think this is now one of the finest floats on the market—I really rate this one.

22. These floats are now used for bleak and small fish in the top 2–3ft of water. Bleaking has changed a bit over the last couple of years, and I learnt this from the Italians. Again these are little Ignesti floats; the shotting pattern, as you can see is, no. 1 the Styl leads for when the fish are taking just under the surface. Before I go any further I should add that they are both 'fishing to hand' rigs, for speed.

When feeding a lot of sloppy groundbait, the other pattern, no. 2, with the bulk shot, which, as you can see, is no. 10's bulked together as near as three inches from the hook. This is fine when the bites are very hard to hit—you do not miss any bites. When bleak fishing this style you watch for any movement on the float ie., float lifting to one side, lifting slightly or simply going under. I also like to have these floats dotted very, very low in the water—say only an $\frac{1}{8}''$ showing.

If you do get problems with the float sinking just too low, all you need to do is just dip the bristle into a jar of Vaseline, and this will make it stand up in the water an extra $\frac{1}{4}''$ if necessary. This is worth remembering for all types of pole fishing with bristle floats—it is a good tip.

The Styl leads are put on with Styl pincers. Place the lead flat with the groove downwards, and pick it up carefully with the pincers. Place it over the line and squeeze very lightly onto the line. The lead can be slid up and down.

The Olivettes I like to use are tungsten and the best on the market I have found to be Clarke's and the Bob Nudd Olivettes.

Before I go any further I'd like to mention that I do not use Olivettes from $\frac{1}{2}$ gm under. I much prefer to use no. 10 shots, bulked together, rather than the lighter Olivettes. I learnt this trick from Michael Crime, you can move the shots according to how the fish are taking and at the same time they are also cheaper. I really think they are better.

22

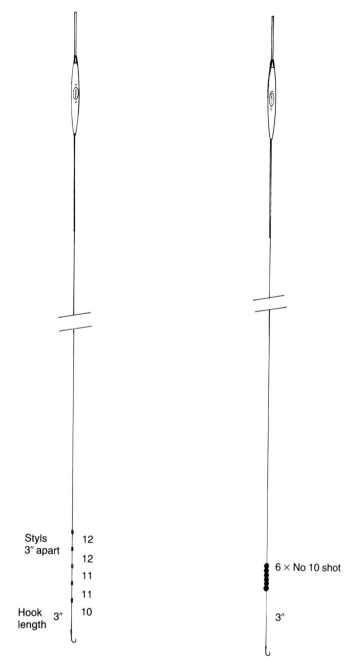

Styls
3″ apart

12

12

11

11

Hook
length

3″

10

6 × No 10 shot

3″

Hooks

I fell in love with the Tubertini hooks. I find Series 1 very good for pinkie, squatt and bloodworm fishing. I found these hooks absolutely unbeatable and people such as Ivan Marks and Bob Nudd agree with this.

The hook I use for bread punch fishing is again a Tubertini Series 4. The line I've found particularly good for hook lengths is Tubertini Superstar nylon. It is graded in millums (0.6 for example). I've found that for pole fishing the 0.6 is first class. One thing I've found extremely useful is the instant Lure Paint Pen by Fisherman's Edge. This is excellent for colouring bristles and is the brightest paint of this kind I've come across.

Roach Fishing

On canals, there seems to have been a roach explosion, and at certain times of the year, the roach do not respond to groundbait, so we have started to use jokers in what we call 'leem'. For this method I've found it best to fish with Styl leads in float No. 21, and either throw the joker in with a small amount of leem, or on windy bays, I prefer to use a pole pot.

Winders in Set Lengths

Colour	Length of line in metres	8 cm	10 cm	Length of Winders 12 cm	14 cm	16 cm	18 cm
Yellow	3.00	23	18	14	12	10	9
Orange	3.30	25	19	16	13	11	10
Green	3.60	28	21	17	14	12	11
Red	3.90	30	23	18	15	13	12
Blue	4.20	32	25	20	17	14	13
Black	5.00	38	29	24	20	17	15

Numbers are the numbers of complete turns round the winder.

Attach an elastic band to the end of the line so this will stretch to the next peg on the winder.

Please remember — litter loses fishing

Fishing Methods and Bait Variations

Bloodworm

Bloodworm fishing has become popular in the south of the country during the past few years, because of their use in the Winter Leagues, Nationals etc., so I will try to describe how best to fish them.

When writing about float no. 5 I said a little about how I fished them for bream, and in deeper water, but in shallower water and for other species they should be fed in a fine groundbait of one of the types already mentioned. Take a pinch of bloodworms, drop it straight onto the groundbait in the bowl, and feed as regularly as possible—say a ball every minute, about the size of a fingernail or a one pence piece. Another good way when roach fishing is to put the bloodworms in neat, with no groundbait at all. Now you might ask me how to do this, so I will tell you the way I find best. Sieve the bloodworms to get them clean, then scatter a little flour over them. This makes it easy to take a pinch of the bloodworms and roll them into little balls to throw in.

For roach fishing, a single bloodworm on the hook seems to work best, while bream seem to like them in twos and threes. This method of feeding works well for gudgeon, perch, and small bream also. Perch don't mind how many bloodworm there are on the hook, although gudgeon seem to prefer a single one.

For this sort of fishing I always use the 5713/5715 hooks because they are a light, very fine wire hook which do not damage the bloodworm when you put them on. The bloodworm should always be hooked through the head, which is the darkest bit at the top. They should not curl up on the hook, but should always hang straight, so straighten them out before casting. If you hook them in the wrong way they will curl up. I often put a piece of red Mystic paste round the shank of the hook when using bloodworms, as the fish seem to like this; it is the same colour as the bloodworm, and it hides the hook completely.

Bloodworms are best kept in an insulated bait box to keep them

The bloodworm box conveniently placed in the hookbait tray.

at an even temperature. The lid of the box should not go right back when it opens, so that it is easier to close, and the inside of the box and lid is lined with polystyrene. Inside the lid, so that it is visible when you open it, you can put a motto or reminder, such as 'don't forget to use a caster occasionally!'

Always keep the lid shut, so the bloodworm will not be damaged by heat or frost.

Bread Punch Fishing

Earlier I have described how to prepare bread punch bait and ground-bait, so now I will give some information on how to fish it. It is surprising how much bread you will get through when bread punch fishing, as you need to feed every cast, or every minute at least, to keep a cloud in the area. If you have prepared the bait properly, you will see that when you throw it in, it will float for two or three seconds before it starts to break up.

Have a good piece of wood with you on which to punch the bread, and to save time I always saw a piece off the side of the bread punch so that I can put the hook in the bread, and it doesn't catch on the side of the punch when I pull it out.

CORRECT BLOODWORM MOUNTING

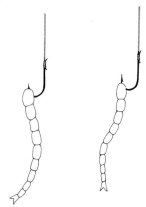

I use the same hooks that I have recommended for bloodworm fishing; I do find these to be very efficient hooks. Bread punches come in three sizes, and for bread from the smallest you will need a size 26 hook, and for the largest a size 20, and only trial and error will tell you which size bread is best. If it happens to be raining, make sure you keep your bread dry. In summer, take out only one prepared slice at a time, or it will dry out in the sun.

Squats and Gozzers

After breeding and preparing the squats and gozzers, use the gozzers as hookbaits and the squats as groundbait. Gozzers go very well when fished over squats but remember that gozzers are very soft and so are easily burst and damaged, so use a fine wire hook. The gozzers should be hooked between the two vents, as with maggots, and are fished either singly or in twos. They are normally fished on the bottom for bream and small roach. Yellow gozzers are worth trying as well as the pure white ones.

Pinkies

Pinkies are one of the commonest forms of maggot used, especially for small fish. They can be used in various colours such as bronze, rhodamine, yellow and white, and they are particularly useful for small fish

Dickie showing young Scott Jenkins the way with the pole after a match win.

where bloodworms are banned and are much used by young anglers. They are very effective baits when loose feeding, with no groundbait required. They are small, so the same pattern of fine wire hook will be needed. Again the bait should be hooked between the vents; the only time when any type of maggot should be hooked differently is through the middle when you are missing bites; here a different method of hooking is worth trying to see if it makes any difference.

Casters

Caster fishing is mainly for quality fish and this bait seems to sort out the better fish, but casters are a much 'slower' bait. They seem to work well on canals, fishing the far bank with the 10-metre pole, and using float no. 14 with a fairly short line. To fish the far bank this way, fire over three or four casters at a time for a while, and then leave for about half an hour. The pole will then reach across to the far bank of many canals and you will normally get instant bites. If you don't get fish within three or four minutes, the fish are not there, or at least are not feeding, so give it up and try later.

Many anglers like to put a towel over the casters to keep them all the same colour, but I prefer to have mine in slightly different colours.

The hookbait tray fitted to the front of the seat.

Redworms

I do not have much to add to what I have already said about fishing with redworms, but it is necessary to say that when using them to catch quality fish I hook them by the head (thick) end and I thread them down the hook, so that the point of the hook projects from the worm lower down from where I have hooked it. If you are missing bites, or you are after small fish, try hooking the worms through the centre.

Different baits sink at different speeds, and a test gave these interesting results.

Sinking Rate of Baits in Seconds per Foot

Pale Casters 8 sec. Dark Casters 10 sec. Large Maggots $7\frac{1}{2}$ sec. Pinkies 13 sec. Loose bloodworms 12 sec. Jokers 14–20 sec. Hemp $4\frac{1}{2}$ sec. *(Test and results supplied by Don Neish, of Don's of Edmonton.)*

How to Play Fish on the Pole

I feel I must say a little about the methods of playing fish on the pole. When *striking* remember that with pole fishing the length of line

Concentration is needed at all times during a match.

from pole tip to float is generally shorter than when using rod and line and therefore only a short, sharp sideways strike is all that is required to set the hook. When fishing running water, strike gently upstream. On still waters strike away from the float in a gentle but firm movement. This is all that is needed. Always try to avoid striking too fiercely, as this can lead to tangles and the possible breakage of the hook length.

When a big fish is first hooked the power of the first run is absorbed by the stretch of the elastic. If this first run can be controlled, the fish will almost certainly be landed safely, but the spare sections of the pole must be close to you so that as the fish runs, you can add the sections of the pole quickly to 'keep up' with the fish. Once all the sections have been added, play the fish on the long pole and try to tire it before you start to remove the sections again. As you slide the pole back through your hands try not to let it vibrate, or you may shake the fish off, so take your time. When the fish is played out, drag it gently across the landing net, which should always have been left in the right position so that it can be reached easily. When playing a big fish on the pole it is a good idea to ask any people who might be behind you not to move about, as any sudden moves may frighten the fish.

Dickie's float selection, 90% of which are home-made and are now also available, bearing his name, at most good tackle shops.

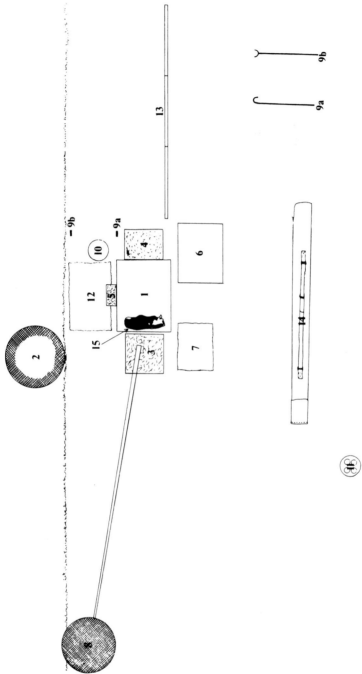

The diagram above shows how I would normally arrange my tackle when fishing a match.
1. Seat; 2. Keepnet; 3. Bait tray; 4. Groundbait bowl; 5. Hookbait tray; 6. Tackle box; 7. Nylon carrier bag (for reserve bait, etc.); 8. Landing net resting on bait tray; 9a. Rear rod rest; 9b. Front rod rest; 10. Bowl of water (for groundbait mixing); 11. Pole holder; 12. Piece of old carpet, for use in winter; 13. Remaining sections of pole when not in use; 14. Rod holdall (positioned to keep spectators back); 15. Piece of rag.

I advise netting fish above 3 ozs rather than trying to lift them on the light tackle normally used for this type of fishing. To save time I sometimes drag fish of up to ½lb in, and lift them by hand, after taking off the appropriate sections of the pole. The longer the line in use the longer the landing net handle should be.

Lastly, I advise trying to pull the fish away from the baited area when it is first hooked, to avoid scaring other fish in the area.

International Pole Fishing Techniques

I now would like to say a little about how match anglers from different countries fish. Anglers from each country seem to specialise in different methods and techniques. The Germans use large floats for their deep canals. The floats are also heavy and are fished on poles of 10–12 metres with the same amount of line, and the swinging to hand method is used. Twelve to sixteen Olivettes are used to weigh the float and this method works very well owing to the nature of the German waters. The Germans have certainly mastered this method, as they proved when the World Championships were fished in their country. This is not a good system in this country, but it can be used successfully in Ireland.

At the opposite end of the scale, the Italian small fish specialists and noted speed merchants can catch three hundred fish an hour on their short two metre poles and small floats. When the fish are further out they use their ten-metre poles with ten metres of line. Their poles are 'floppy' compared with the stiffer poles used by the Germans.

Now we come to the French, who are undoubtedly the best pole anglers in the world, as their record in numerous World Championships has proved. They fish mainly for small fish with long poles and short lines, although they are also experts at landing even four- and five-pound fish.

The English have not really specialised, but seem to like to try a bit of everything. They use the German type methods in Ireland, with the Italian style for bleak and other small fish here in the UK, whilst long poles and short lines as used by the French are very popular in England at the moment. This approach has brought considerable success and England have been very consistent in the World Championships. In addition to winning on three occasions, they have had several individual winners including Ian Heaps, Dave Thomas, Tom Pickering, Dave Roper and Kevin Ashurst.

More English anglers are now going to Ireland for matches and there were more in the Irish Festivals in May 1983 than I have ever seen. Ian Heaps and I gained a lot of useful knowledge about bream in Ireland recently. We used big floats like the Germans do, no. 7 in the strong flow found in Irish rivers, and we cast downstream with the float slightly

Sometimes it is an advantage to position yourself actually in the water although
this will often stop the fish from coming close in.

over-shotted. We held onto the floats, letting them push round at the
end of the swim, with three or four floating casters on size twelve hooks.
This way, with good presentation, we had many bream up to $3\frac{1}{2}$lb. Many
anglers are still using worms, but the fish are getting wise to them, and
those intending to go to Ireland to fish might do well to remember that
dark casters may be the best baits.

When bloodworm fishing on the River Lea in the Tottenham area,
which is infested with sticklebacks, I have found that the key to doing
well on matches here is to avoid the sticklebacks and minnows, and one
way I have found to do this is to use a lot of peat in the groundbait.
I keep a bowl of this groundbait and throw in handfuls of white groundbait
in peat. I have found that the small fish prefer to stay in the clear water
and are nervous of going into the groundbait 'cloud' whilst perch and
roach move into the cloud to feed. My success in a number of matches
at this venue was due to avoiding the sticklebacks this way—a tip I have
kept to myself until now!

This photograph shows the different light conditions that can occur from one side of the river to the other. Here the colour of the float may need to be changed if you vary the fishing range.

The correct way to hold the pole.

Perch Fishing

Over the last couple of years on certain canals where bloodworm has been banned and there is not a big head of roach, perch fishing in matches has really come into its own. People have developed and worked on the best way to get the most perch out of your swim: they've come up with what we call 'the chopped worm method'.

For this you need at least five or six lobworms: the best way to get them is to go out with a torch, late at night, preferably on a dampish night, and grab them as they lie on the surface—you need a few small redworms as well. Now you've got your bait, you need a general canal float, type 21 and fish it slightly overdepth, but you must keep jerking it and moving it all the time.

Let me explain how to go about this method. First of all, you must have a pole pot for the end of your pole; cut up a lobworm into $\frac{1}{4}''$ pieces, and drop them in your pole pot, and fish over them. I think it is the smell from the chopped worm which attracts the perch and the daddy ruffe.

I like to use about a size 20 or 22 hook and for bait I either use a small worm, or a $\frac{1}{4}''$ piece of chopped worm. You will be surprised how successful this method can be. Before I finish, I will stress again the importance of keeping the hook bait moving.

Gudgeon Rigs

Gudgeon fishing is becoming very popular on canals like the Oxford Canal, and it is surprising how many matches are won with gudgeon. Most good weights of gudgeon are caught on a three- or four-metre pole, fishing to hand. What I have learnt is that you can fish as much as $1\frac{1}{2}$ gm of weight of the float for gudgeon and also have the Olivette as near as four inches to the hook. This does sound very crude but it is important to get the bait down as quickly as possible, and the bites are then instant. It is also important to get the depth just right—normally just touching bottom is about right, but you can vary it an inch or two either way.

You also at times catch a lot more fish using a bottom end on the pole with an Olivette down, especially in bad wind conditions. Also it is advisable to use very small hooks—I prefer the Tubertini series 1, in size 26. If you are using bloodworm and joker, it is often worth putting a joker on the hook, and you will keep catching. Feeding is very important—but I will discuss that in one of the matches I am going to tell you about later.

BEWARE

OVERHEAD ELECTRIC POWER LINES

WARNING!

Living for fishing is one thing. Dying for it, or maiming yourself for life, is quite another. The one blot on the history and development of pole fishing in the last decade has been the number of serious accidents involving poles and overhead power lines.

The new carbon poles are frighteningly efficient at conducting electricity. They are long enough nowadays to make contact with power lines, but they do not even need to connect. Get one near enough and the power arcs across, with devastating results.

Fellow anglers have been killed. Two friends of ours have been horribly burned, and one has lost part of a leg. It should never have happened; it cannot happen to you or to us? But of course it can, unless you and we take the greatest of care.

So obey warning notices, and the advice from the electricity generating industry and the National Federation of Anglers to LOOK OUT and LOOK UP whenever you even think about setting up pole tackle in an area you are not familiar with.

Perhaps the reason why "lightning" never strikes twice is that it does not usually have to....

PLEASE DON'T DIE FOR YOUR FISHING!

Pole Fishing Experiences

One Man's Match—by Dickie Carr

I thought that it might be interesting to readers of this book to tell the story in detail of one particular match in which I fished, out of the hundreds in which I have taken part.

The one I have chosen is the Barnet Open at London Colney in Hertfordshire, in which 140 anglers took part. London Colney is a big lake set in a bird sanctuary and there are 140 pegs on the lake. I decided to fish this match only a week before it took place because I had had to cancel my tickets to the two-day Rother Open due to a Captain Morgan Knockout cup match which clashed with the first day of the Rother Open. I phoned Eric Kent to see if he could get me a ticket for the Barnet Match, and he said that he would be able to get me one from a Committee member who was not taking part.

I didn't have long to prepare for this match, and I had never fished the lake before, although I had seen it when I went there to give some help to some youngsters. I realised then that there were a lot of small bream and tench there, which responded well to a nice cloud, so I decided that I would fish mainly for skimmers. My bait was to be gozzers which I had bred myself, with squats in the groundbait, which I flavoured with vanilla for the sweet-toothed bream. I also coloured the groundbait red with a food dye, as I knew that I would then have a different coloured groundbait from the others who were fishing the match.

I arrived and drew peg no. 86, and was immediately told that this was not really in a fancied area, although there were a few bream about. When I reached my peg I found it to be under some trees, with the wind in my face. This is usually a good sign on lakes. Owing to the trees above, I realised that the pole would be best, so I tackled up with a ten-metre pole, float no. 15 attached to the bottom end only, and an 8oz bottom with a size 26 hook, pattern no. 5713. I mixed up my groundbait very wet to make a complete cloud, added the squats, and waited for the whistle to go.

At the start I plumbed the depth and found that I had nine feet of water in front of me at a distance of ten metres. I started to feed cloud groundbait at regular intervals, putting it in carefully just past the float, so that I could take fish off the near edge of the cloud, without having to drag fish through the baited area. I set the tackle so that the bait was just half an inch from the bottom and the float so that bites would register if the bait was taken on the drop.

I went for 30 minutes without a bite, then had a couple of small roach on a small red gozzer, so I kept feeding steadily. Soon I started to catch a few small skimmer bream in the 4–8oz bracket, and then I hooked a tench of about 1¼lb, which gave me a few frights on the very light tackle before I finally netted it. The bream kept coming and although in the next hour I lost two good tench I soon realised that I was well on target with the bream for a weight of between 12 and 16lb, which I thought might be enough to win, so I was quite happy to continue catching the bream.

By this time some young boys were sitting with me telling me that not much was being caught, so it looked good so far. For the rest of the match I fed and caught steadily, maintaining a reasonable catch rate, although I did have to keep altering the depth at which I fished as I found that some of the skimmers tended to rise off the bottom. I am convinced that my different coloured groundbait did help a lot on that day, and so, apparently, did others, for since that match red groundbait has been commonly used at that lake, even though it was little or never used before.

When the scales came round at the end of the match, I thought I had about 12lb, but my final weight was 15lb 3oz, which was made up of two tench, four or five little roach and the rest skimmer bream. However, I heard that someone had caught seven big bream on the ledger towards the end of the match, so I wasn't confident that I had enough to win, but on my return to Headquarters I was quickly informed that I had won by about a pound, which was very satisfying, and which completed a double for me that weekend.

For winning this match I received a beautiful cup, and the match raised over £100 for disabled anglers.

I consider this one of the most interesting matches I have fished in as I had put a lot of thought and effort into planning for the match in the short time I had available, and everything went to plan. My success here also goes to show, as I have been trying to emphasise throughout this book, how important it is for the pole angler to try something different—but this year I definitely won't be using red groundbait at London Colney!

Dickie is well known for helping youngsters, especially after matches, but this time the 'order of the day' appears to be autographs.

Four out of Four—by Richard Borley

This story relates to four matches in the eight days between July 15th and 23rd 1977. Three of these matches were at Wyboston on the Middle Ouse and the other was on the Rive Lea at Broxbourne. The most important factors affecting the outcome of these matches were bright sunshine and a lack of wind. These two combined to put the larger fish off the feed and leave the way clear for an angler fishing for bleak to win. As I fished for bleak throughout all four matches I think it would be useful initially to set out the tackle and methods used.

First I will explain the layout of my secondary tackle; although this is more a matter of personal choice one must realise that 'bleaking' as it is commonly referred to, is not solely a matter of bait presentation, but speed is of the essence. It is quite possible for two anglers to sit side by side and catch a fish every cast and one will weigh in five pounds while the other has ten pounds. The first thing to do is to get comfortable and when bleaking this usually involves sitting as close to the water as possible, especially as we are trying to catch as close in as possible so the angler must remain out of his fishes' field of vision. Once this is achieved I place my keepnet directly underneath my unhooking hand, be it left or right, so that the fish can be swung straight over the net and dropped into it as quickly as possible. Next I put a bait tray just to the left of my left knee. This holds my loose feed, hookbait, spare hooks and shot and as I feed with my left hand and hold the pole with my right I am wasting no time. Lastly I position my spare pole usually behind me so that I can interchange the two with the minimum of fuss.

When one breaks down a typical bleak match into figures it becomes obvious that it really is a 'time and motion' exercise. To catch 10lb of bleak in a five-hour match on most venues involves hooking, landing and unhooking between 450 and 500 fish in 300 minutes. When taking into account that one also has to feed, usually around five pints of maggots (about 15,000) throwing in no more than 15 at a time and that you will probably average two casts per fish, maybe more, if broken down further in each hour of the contest you will cast out 200 times, feed 200 times, strike 200 times, unhook 100 fish and rebait probably 30–40 times, not to mention altering your tackle or changing between poles! From this you will see that bleak fishing is no lazy man's sport.

The actual tackle used is again designed with speed in mind. I invariably set up two poles, both of the same make. These are light fibre-glass poles with a thin flexible top joint so that you don't 'bump' any fish on the strike. One pole is 10 feet long and the other is 14 feet. To the end of each pole I tie a length of five pound line and then an 18-inch hooklength of one pound line, culminating in a size 20 barbless hook, which may be changed depending on the catch rate. The length of line

Richard Borley with the *Sun* 'Kingfisher' Stan Piecha and a catch of bream from
Lake Triel, Paris, taken on long poles.

has to be such that when a fish is swung in, it comes straight to your left hand. The reason for the relatively thick top line is because you grease a four foot section of this between your hook-length knot and a one-inch piece of plastic or peacock quill so that it floats. When a fish takes your bait the greased line will disappear underneath the surface starting with the knot, thus affording the fish the least possible resistance. The only shot on the line varies between one and three number 10's depending on conditions and the confidence of the bites.

Before we come on to the use of the tackle and the method of feeding, I feel I must give credit for the formulation of some of the ideas and methods explained here to Brian Bailey who is captain of Bromage Match-mates, the club I belonged to at the time of these matches.

The first of the three matches at Wyboston was on the Saturday and when I arrived at the venue the river looked like a mill pool, and this was what first gave me the idea of fishing for bleak. However, when I drew peg 18 in the big meadow I was not so sure, as this was a good draw for skimmers in normal conditions, the best bleak pegs being from 25 to 30 where the river bends and the flow is right under your feet. When I got to my peg I set up a waggler and two poles in the way I have described. The whistle went at 10 o'clock and I started on the pole. Previous experience told me that the best way to feed for bleak involves baiting the whole area that can be covered by your poles on the little and often principle. In other words, you do not try to get the fish packed too tightly in front of you and risk scaring them too quickly, but try and pick up two or three fish from all over the swim. Using this method I started to catch fairly regularly but as the flow was down the middle of the river and there was no wind at all the fish wouldn't stay close in for long periods. For hookbait I used bronze pinkies which proved more successful that a big maggot; whether this was because a pinkie plus the weight of the hook sinks at the same pace as a loose fed bronze maggot, I don't know, but the bites were more confident on a pinkie with the greased line slowly sinking until you struck, whereas on a big maggot the greased section would give a lightning twitch and then stop. At the end of the match I thought I had about five pounds, enough for a section win but did not dream I had enough to win. As it turned out I weighed in 6lb 5 oz and the second weight was 3lb 7oz.

When I arrived for the draw for the 125-peg open match on Sunday at Wyboston again and saw that the weather conditions were identical to the previous day, I knew bleak would be the only quarry. Three of us had travelled together to the match and I drew the best peg of the three, number 27, right in the middle of the best bleak area. Using the same methods as the previous day I caught well all day, swapping between the long and short pole and getting through six pints of loose feed. The only difference I found to the previous day was that when the bites slowed

I would pick up two or three large bleak by putting a red pinkie on the hook before having to change back to a bronze sample. Why this was I do not pretend to know but it certainly worked. At the weigh-in I knew I had topped the 6lb 5oz of Saturday, but was surprised to put 9lb 14oz (450 bleak) on the scales. My two travelling companions Brian Bailey (7lb 7oz) and Mick Hood (6lb 13oz) were second and third. So with two wins in two days I was extremely happy, not to say confident on this particular venue.

The third match was a Tuesday evening sweepstake on the River Lea at Broxbourne, and with the same weather conditions prevailing I took a gamble and ignored the usual chub tactics, setting up my usual two bleak poles. At the end of the two and three quarter hours I had put together 3lb 1oz of bleak and small roach caught in exactly the same way as the two previous matches, with over half of my fish coming on the red pinkie. This time I really felt I had not caught enough to win, but to my surprise the chub had kept their mouths closed and I had won three out of three. It is a strange thing in match fishing but it is often the case, that when you think you have no chance of winning with what you have weighed in, you often do, and conversely when you are confident that you have done enough you sometimes get pipped. One of the worst moments in match angling is waiting at the headquarters after the match and hearing any other weights come in to beat you. It is great when your name is called out first but you get a sick feeling when you get beaten by a weight that you had not heard of.

On the next Saturday I drove to Wyboston in a confident mood but when I got to the river the bright sunshine was still there but a strong upstream wind was putting a considerable ripple on the water. I thought that this was the time the roach and skimmers could feed. I drew peg 84, an area I had not previously fished and set up tackle for skimmers as well as my usual bleak tackle. Just before the whistle blew the wind dropped, so I started for bleak, catching well for an hour on the long pole. At this time the wind got up again and started putting a big ripple in an upstream direction and I stopped catching. I reasoned that the wind was blowing my light tackle upstream, pulling the hookbait against the flow causing my bait to look unnatural to the fish. To counter this I put another number 10 shot on my hooklength to get it underneath the wind. I started to catch a few more fish but not fast enough. In desperation I put a number eight right next to the spade of my hook, cast in and got a fish straight away, followed by one after another. Quickly I swapped to the short pole, altered the tackle accordingly and caught steadily till the end of the match. I finished up weighing in 7lb 15oz and was confident of getting in the frame or winning if the skimmers had not shown. I had a long walk back to the headquarters from my peg and was told I had won as soon as I had arrived. Four wins in four successive matches and a couple of smashing trophies as well.

The Little Ouse Championship—by Mick Burrell

Having come in the top four on the three previous matches on this venue my confidence was sky high. The peg I drew, no. 34, had no previous form but one of my team mates Jeff Forman had drawn close to it on the match before; he told me that the streamer weed in that area was very bad and that I was about three pegs off a 'flyer'. When I arrived at my peg I was amazed at the amount of weed. It was so thick from under my feet to the far bank. The water was gin clear but had a fair push on it. About eight metres out I noticed a very small run, only about a foot wide and six or seven feet long; this was the only fishable area I had.

My previous success on the river had all been due to the pole fished with bread punch and this match was to be no exception. The pole I used has four joints. This enables me to make up two different set-ups, one of which has a reversed crow quill fished bottom end. This was locked in with 2BB shot and had three no. 10's strung out down the line. The other one was a small bristle float which also carried two BB and three no. 10's. The 2BB were used as a bulk placed about two feet from the hook and the tens were evenly spaced below that. The hooks used were size twenty tied to 12oz bottoms on both rigs. The only other set-up was a ledger rod which was to be used as a last resort for eels. Groundbait was next. I used just ordinary white crumb mixed very wet. Having laid out all my gear I decided to have a look at the 'flyer' peg Jeff had told me about. It was in fact four pegs below mine and looked a tremendous swim with a long glide running right through thick streamer weed. Roach could be seen swimming in and out of the weed. The chap who had drawn this peg told me it had produced the winner in a club match the week before. Wishing him luck I walked back to my own peg just in time for the whistle. I clipped a plummet on the crow quill set-up and found the swim to be about four feet deep with thick blanket weed on the bottom. Putting a piece of punch on the hook and casting into the channel the float dragged under straight away. I dropped the float six inches. The float still dragged under; the problem was that the hook was getting caught on unseen streamer weed. There was only one answer. I would have to hold back and ease the float through the swim. This meant changing to the top and bottom bristle float. Moving the bulk shot right under the float and spacing out the tens made the float fish much better. After a short while came the first fish, a small roach about three inches long. This was followed by a few more fish of the same size. Feeding small balls of groundbait every cast I noticed that now and then the small fry would scatter right in the middle of the cloud and the fish would then disappear for about ten minutes. It was obvious that I had a pike in my swim.

By this time the fish were getting smaller and fewer, but I kept the groundbait going in every cast hoping for some bigger fish to turn up. Then the swim went dead; nothing happened for half an hour. It was time for a change. I replaced the size 20 hook with a 24 and changed the $\frac{3}{4}$lb breaking strain bottom to one of half a pound. I pushed the float and bulk shot up the line another six inches and cast in again. I let the float travel down the swim at about half the speed of the current, and this change in tactics brought an immediate bite. This was a much better fish of about 4oz, and it was followed by three more of about the same size. I looked at my watch; one hour to go. I looked back at my float just in time to see it go under. I had hooked another roach. As I passed the pole back, the tip suddenly jerked violently, and I realised a pike had taken the hooked roach. As I reached for my spare pole joint the pike went solid in the weed, and I just held on, not daring to pull. I could see the pike lying about two feet under the surface, and suddenly it started to come towards me, breaking surface about fifteen feet out.

Amazingly, the pike kept coming. I put the landing net in—and it swam straight into it, with the roach still in its mouth. I forced the mouth open with a rag and managed to get the roach out, so I put them both in the keep net; the roach swam off, not seeming to be hurt badly.

I fished the rest of the match without another bite. At the scales I weighed in $4\frac{1}{2}$lb, and was pleased to find that I had won the section. The first person I saw was Jeff, who said that mine was the best weight he had heard of, and that I was in with a good chance of winning. When I got back to headquarters I found that I had won by about $1\frac{1}{4}$lb.

Although I know that it is not really a good thing to win a match with the help of a pike, I can't help thinking that I would certainly have caught much more if the pike had not been in my swim in the first place.

Fishing for England—by Dickie Carr

I was fortunate enough to be selected to fish for England in the 1977 World Championships in Luxembourg, and this was undoubtedly my greatest moment.

The team was to have a week's practice in Luxembourg first, and Ivan Marks and I arranged to travel down to Dover together and meet the others there. Unfortunately, we got lost on the way down and arrived just as the boat was due to sail. We were in such a hurry that we actually finished up on the wrong boat and ended up in France instead of Belgium. It was 2.00pm before we arrived in Luxembourg, worn out and feeling very foolish at having started off so badly.

The week's fishing practice was hard work, although I enjoyed it. Stan Smith, the Manager, had us up at 6.00am every morning, and we fished from 8.00am till 6.00pm every day. The river was very wide with a fast flow and an average depth of 12 feet. As we had no carbon poles in those days, we had to fish very hard with our fibre glass poles, and it was usually 1.00am before we got back to the hotel.

Two weeks later we were back again for the World Championship. One of us had to be reserve, and I was desperately hoping, as no doubt were all the others, that it wouldn't be me. After one more practice session, just above the match length, the team was announced—and I was in!

I shall never forget this match. The atmosphere and pressure of a World Championship is indescribable. We all felt nervous when we settled down in the ten-yard area allotted to us. We were allowed to sit anywhere in that ten yards, but could not feed, or cast, out of it. The ten-minute pre-baiting period just before the match was incredible. Some of the teams put 30 cricket-ball-sized lumps of groundbait into their swim in that time. Each competitor has a steward behind him, which does not happen in English matches, and this makes for even greater pressure. The steward has to mark down each fish you catch, and you have to call out and hold up the fish every time you catch one. You get a point for each fish, and a point for every gram of weight.

In spite of the tension I felt that I did quite well, as I caught 49 fish—gudgeon, bleak and roach—and finished sixth in my section out of 18. The local Luxembourg team won the Championships using ten or eleven metre carbon poles, with a short line. All their bloodworms and groundbait were put in before the match started, and their hook bait was Mystic paste and two bloodworms. The English team came fifth.

Fishing for England in a World Championship must be the peak of achievement of any match angler, and I was again picked for the England team in 1983.

First place again—this time 27-15 of bream (up to 5-12) at the ABU Spectacular,
Coombe Abbey Lake, Coventry.

World Match Record—by Peter Burrell

As has now become customary at the Benson and Hedges Festival Week (now the Ulster Classic), Billy Knott held an open invitation match on the River Sillees on the second rest day.

As this is a small length of river, only 32 pegs were allocated, from which I drew peg 8, positioned at the bottom end of a pool created by a small weir. The swim looked ideal, for at seven metres there was a slack created by an eddy, and then the flow suddenly increased as you came towards the back, where it was quite fast and turbulent. From what I had learned in the England v. Ireland invitation match fished on the same length on the first rest day, the fish were definitely in the flow and although this particular swim had not produced a match winning weight before, I felt sure that if I could get the fish to feed in the fast flow under the bank, I had a good chance of winning.

I set up four poles, of five metres, four metres, and two at three metres long, so that if the fish were to move in close I had a back-up rig ready in case of line breakage. Each pole had a very stiff top joint, to which I attached a short length of 6lb line to act as a shock absorber, for, as previous experience had shown, the most likely place for a breakage to occur is where the line meets the pole tip. Connected to this was 4lb breaking strain line which was tied direct to a size 12 eyed hook, which would help to prevent the maggots from blowing up the line. The floats were very short, consisting of a balsa body tapering off to a thin bristle insert, and they each took just over $1\frac{1}{2}$ swan shot. They were connected to the line top and bottom and 3AAA shot were positioned about 22cm from the hook with a number 8 shot acting as a dropper below the bulk shot, and a number 6 under the float to lock it into position. My intention was that the bulk shot would get the bait down quickly, and the dropper shot, in conjunction with the bristle insert, would enable me to see the bites early to minimise damage to the maggot, thus allowing several fish to be caught on the same bait.

Because of the speed of the water, groundbait was essential to ensure that the feed reached the bottom of my swim, so I mixed up two very large bowls which consisted mainly of brown crumb, with a little white to bind it, two gallons of casters and one gallon of maggots.

Plumbing the depth at the start of the match showed that at three metres the water was $1\frac{1}{2}$ metres deep, increasing to three metres in depth at a distance of five metres. I placed three large balls of groundbait in the fast water on the near side, squeezed to make them break near the bottom. I then placed three more balls in the slower water further out, getting these to break in mid water, and I started fishing at this distance, baiting with three bronze maggots.

It took a few minutes for the first fish to come and then slowly but surely the bites started coming faster, with about 30 fish being caught in the first half hour. During this period I only fed the closer area, still hoping that the fish would move in and knowing that I needed to catch an average of 90 per hour to stand any chance in the match, I now decided to try the short pole. I found there were fish close in, although initially they weren't coming very much faster than before, but I persevered and continued to feed small balls of groundbait which eventually had the desired effect, because the end of the first hour had shown the catch rate increasing considerably with a fish count of 98. The second hour proved to be even better, for I had built up a good catching rhythm, and I put another 175 roach and perch in the net in the hour.

The third hour turned out to be the climax of the day, with fish coming in short sharp bursts of up to seven a minute, or so I was told afterwards, and it was only now I realised that not only did I have a chance of winning the match, but also of breaking the world record if I could keep up the same catch rate for the remaining two hours.

However, I soon found, to my dismay, that the bites were slowing down, and on searching my swim it became evident that the fish were moving downstream away from me. I continued to catch at a much reduced speed on the four-metre pole, and then the five metre, as the roach dropped further down the swim, and I could see my chances slipping away.

A remedy had to be found, and quickly, and in thinking over my actions in the past $3\frac{1}{2}$ hours I realised that my feed must have moved further down the swim, taking the fish with it. The reason suddenly became clear; I had become so engrossed in catching fish as fast as I could that I had failed to notice that the water flow had become faster. My immediate reaction was to stop feeding, and slowly the fish came closer, but now I had to try to keep them where they were, and to prevent them going straight past me to the guy upstream. I adjusted the groundbait mix, stiffening it considerably and then placed two more balls into the swim. These had to be squeezed quite hard to prevent them from splitting until they had reached the bottom.

It worked, and by continuing to feed the stiff mix, I kept the roach in the swim, and the catch rate steadily increased again, although it never reached the peak I had achieved in the third hour.

I had worked harder in that five hours than I had ever done before, on or off the bank, and I was very relieved when the final whistle blew. I had landed 782 roach and perch and although I felt that I had done enough to win the match, I was convinced that I was about 20lb short of the existing record, which stood at 209lb. I was so sure of this that when Tom Boulton said: 'I bet you £5 that you've broken it', I had no hesitation in taking the wager.

When the scales arrived, it took six men to lift my nets, and it was

Pete with his amazing record catch weighing 259lb 3¾oz.

only then that I appreciated the size of these fish. That was one bet I did not mind losing, for after the last batch of fish were weighed, the final tally was 117kg 580g. This was converted by the organisers into Imperial weights as 259lb $9\frac{1}{2}$oz, but has subsequently been corrected to 259lb $3\frac{3}{4}$oz—a new world match record.

Unlike English fish, Irish roach are extremely strong and are in prime condition, so I can assure any worried anglers that all the fish were returned alive to the water after being weighed and pictures taken, and to the best of my knowledge, every fish swam away safely.

This is the one match in my career that I will always remember, but in a way I am glad that I do not live in Ireland as I do not think I could afford the bait bills every week, and I also doubt that I would have the energy to fish matches like this very often!

Home Internationals 1983—by Dickie Carr

It might interest readers to hear about the 1983 Internationals which I mentioned earlier in the book. I left early on Thursday morning, 30th June 1983 to get to Holyhead for the 4am boat, and arrived in Dublin at 7.00pm. We rushed straight to the Newry canal to see the match length ready for practice on the Friday and Saturday. We then went to the hotel and had an early night. We were short of bloodworm so Dennis Salmon arranged to have some flown in from Holland; bait for the week-end cost £60 to £80 per man! Everyone was fishing for prestige only, as no money was involved, but I must say that the Irish organisation was first class, both during the match and at the reception afterwards; indeed, I have found all Irish matches to be excellently organised—you couldn't be better looked after when you are in Ireland.

We practised all day on Friday using large floats taking ten to twelve Olivettes with a short line on ten to twelve metre poles. There was more practice on Saturday, and the evening was spent putting on winders and getting everything ready.

The day of the match came and I was very happy with my draw, which was in the 50s, which I was told was a good area. After all that practice I knew exactly how to fish.

The match was run with World Championship ideas; a five minute baiting-up period was allowed and I put in ten balls only, and also plumbed the depth. It was necessary to get the groundbait exactly in the right place, so the plumbing was useful to find out if the bank sloped down and to find the exact level of the bottom. The best way to get this exactly right is to put the float in, using no bait, and to lay the pole in the water. The groundbait balls can then be thrown in exactly where the float would go.

I started to catch after ten minutes, small bream on the twelve metre line. This continued quite steadily. Quite a few youngsters were watching by now, so I invited them to sit beside me, as they were interested to see my bloodworm fishing, which was new to them. In fact, these boys were useful to me, as they started timing the catch rate for me. This was a typical bloodworm venue, and with the float overshotted I was able to lift it and work it, moving it at times just an inch or so to the side which tempts the fish to take.

After $1\frac{1}{2}$ hours the bites were slowing down a bit so I put in another ball of groundbait. I started getting some lift bites as the fish were coming into the groundbait cloud, and at first the youngsters couldn't even see the float moving, but they soon caught on.

By now I had quite a big gallery, which included local Councillors and the organisers as well as the boys, and the cars pulling up were starting to put the fish off! Dennis Salmon got them to move off, though

I was quite happy with the youngsters, who were a great help. The catch rate was 30 fish in the first hour, 30 in the second hour, 31 in the third hour and 29 in the last. I used $3\frac{1}{2}$ feet of elastic through the centre of the pole, as described earlier in chapter two, because those small bream have soft mouths and the elastic softens the action of the pole when pulling the pole behind you, and there is less chance of 'bouncing' the fish off as you pull the pole back. There is a lot of elastic with this system when playing the fish and the use of long poles of this kind favours the elastic through the pole system.

I realised by the end of the match that I had 27–28lb of fish in the net as the youngsters had been counting, and was confident that I would win, although this was not particularly important, the main idea being to win the section as this was a team event, and we had come in order for the team to win. When the scales came I weighed in 27lb 9oz and I was first, and much to my delight our South of England team did win the team event, which made all the long journey and the practising well worth while. The presentation in the evening, as I said earlier, was first class with free drinks, good food and excellent prizes. My prize was a fine Waterford crystal bowl, and I should like to thank the local club for their marvellous organisation.

As can be seen from this story, not all match anglers fish for money or at least not all the time—I gave up a valuable match and it cost me £300 for the Irish trip, but I really enjoyed it as I like the Irish and the Irish matches; there is no doubt whatever that Irish fishing is the best in the world.

The Home Internationals were fished by England, Ireland, Scotland, Wales and a local team, and each team consisted of six members.

Since this I have been lucky enough to fish for England again in the Clive Smith Memorial match and again our England team won, and I am looking forward to the World Championships in Holland in September, where I hope to do well.

British Pole Championships 1988—by Dickie Carr

I've been lucky enough now to have won the British Pole Championship twice in the few years it has been run, and as it is run on heats, semi-finals and finals, this is an achievement I'm very proud of. I will start by telling you how you go about getting into the final.

Through the season there are a number of qualifying matches up and down the country, and the winner of each ten pegs goes through to the semi-final, which considering you only get to fish a couple of matches, I think it is harder to get into the semis than to qualify for the final.

The semis are held in the North and South, over 100 in each, but in the semis, the top 50 from each go through to the final. Our Southern semi is normally held on the River Lea at Stonebridge Lock, which is a home water to me and to be honest a very fair water during the summer months, which makes it reasonably easy for the local angler like myself to qualify. In our semi-final I knew that 3lb would put me into the final, I did not draw particularly well, but I fished bloodworm and joker, and after about $3\frac{1}{2}$ hours I knew I had enough to qualify, so I decided to lay on with caster for the rest of the match to give myself a chance of individual glory; this resulted in me picking up a few quality roach, and losing a 3lb-plus chub, which would have put me in the top three, but the elastic pulled out and the fish kept going. I was very choked at the time because it was a very 'expensive' fish to lose.

When I got back to H/Q the smile was soon back on my face as the partner I share with, Glenn Brown, had weighed in 11lb, to win the match and nearly £500, so I was a happy man. I finished in the top 20 with about 5lb—now for the final!

I went on my own in the final because I was off to Ireland straight after for a months fishing. The night before I scraped myself some fresh joker and also scrounged some big bloodworm from Simon Nicholas. At the draw I drew peg 165 and was told it wasn't a bad area, about five or six pegs from the end. I was very satisfied with my draw. The Gloucester Canal is a very deep venue which I've only fished a couple of times before, but I had been told that you must find some flat bottom and fish that area. I got to my peg and plumbed up the depth and found that at 9am I had a perfectly flat bottom with an ideal depth of ten feet, which gave me a tremendous amount of confidence, because the last peg I fished here was 17ft deep and kept sloping away. I started by putting in three balls of Secret and joker, and proceeded to fish bloodworms on the hook, and also loose feeding a few bronze maggots.

My set-up was a 1gm Dickie Carr pear-shaped float, 1lb main line and a 22 series 1 Tubertini hook to 0.6 hook length, fished just touching bottom. I waited about ten minutes for my first bite, which was a small roach, and then they started to come reasonably steadily. I was still flicking in a few maggots, and also putting in every now and again a very small amount of Secret, mixed with Coolart, which is a binder and which goes down very quickly, then breaks up very quickly, and the fish really responded, and I started to get some better quality ones. I kept trying the bronze maggot but was waiting longer for bites, and only getting the same size fish, so I fished bloodworm for the rest of the match.

There were soon a few people behind me telling me I was in with a chance, as I was catching very well compared with others. I had the feeling the fish would keep coming and that I was going to win—it's funny, but sometimes you know when the fish will keep feeding and I was really enjoying myself, when all of a sudden, with 45 minutes to go, a very large boat came round the bend at full speed! He started to slow down as soon as he saw the anglers. I grabbed my net to make sure it was OK, the water coloured up. and my sport was finished for the day, apart from one small flounder.

The boat slowed down and only really affected the first 10 or 12 anglers on the match length, and a rumour came down the bank that Kim Millstone was catching very well—and all there was to do was to sit there and wonder whether I'd got enough, because there was no doubt that the boat had cost me 2–3lb of fish.

At the end I estimated that I had 11–13lb. I was one of the last to weigh in and was soon informed that Kim had weighed in at 11lb 14oz and that he was probably top. This is when the old senses keep speculating: have I got enough! People kept saying, 'You've definitely got 12lb, Dick'. I thought I did have enough, but you worry—I really wanted that title badly.

The scales came along ... and I weighed in 12lb 10oz; a great relief. It's funny, but when you do well you always get plenty of helpers to get you back with your tackle!

Back at H/Q Glenn Brown had an even bigger smile on his face than I had; his words were: 'You've won it, Dick!'

My reward was the British Pole Championship for the second time in four years, £1,000 in cash (well, £500 for me, £500 for Glenn), a lovely trophy and a £700 pole.

What a way to start my holiday! I was definitely on a high at the time, for three days later I was second in the first Festival in Ireland and another £600 better off—and no shares for Glenn Brown!

King of Clubs Match—by Dickie Carr

The King of Clubs is in Ireland, one of my favourite places. This year they decided to make the first pay-out £5,000 instead of £3,000, but only to peg six competitors instead of 20. This was one of the biggest pay-outs in match fishing, and also one of the main titles to be won, because it took place on a river, a canal and a lake and it was on points as well.

I really wanted to win this one: I had been third the year before and have never been out of the top ten. To win the King of Clubs, though, you must have Lady Luck on your side.

With three venues, the river is the one where you must draw right—and I drew peg no. 1, which was an out-and-out winner. From here I went on to win the day, with 57lb on the pole; second place was less than 30lb. It was an easy match to win, though, because I had the best swim by a mile.

The second day was on the canal, with 150 anglers fishing. You drew to fish in three sections, A, B and C, and you got one day on each venue, with 50 points for last, up to one point for the winner: the one with the least points is the winner. Canals, to be honest, suit me; I like canal fishing. I fished bloodworm and joker on the inside line, and caster on the far bank, again on the pole, and I weighed in 7lb something, for third in section, which put me into the very strong position going into the last day, but with a very hard venue to come.

There is one day's rest before the final match, but all the venues are closed, so you couldn't use them for practice. I spent the day at another lake, making sure that all my rigs were perfect, and then preparing all my bait.

Come the morning, I drew peg no 19; looking at the results for the previous two days I could see there was no form on the peg at all, the highest a 30th position in section. I knew I had a battle on my hands. On getting to the peg, I found photographers there to take photos in anticipation, and also a few spectators.

I decided to put some gear out on the 11-metre line, with bloodworm and joker in beet groundbait, and to fish the close line with pinkies and squats to catch the small roach and rudd which I knew would be there. After two hours I think I had about 3oz and was starting to get despondent, thinking my chance had gone; by the way, so had the photographers, and the people; they'd all left!

I thought I'd do something different, so I put the rest of my jokers and bloodworm in the groundbait, and changed down to a 26 hook and 10oz line to catch some smaller fish to try to stay in the top few positions. After about 20 minutes the float slid away and on striking I realised I was into a good bream, which took me nearly a quarter of an hour to land on the very fine tackle. I don't think I've ever been so happy to see a 4lb bream in my life. Going out again I hooked another straight away, and eventually after a long fight, I got it in the net. The old winning feeling was coming back to me—I was still in with a chance.

I promptly changed to a 1lb hook length and a size 22 hook to catch fish more quickly. In spite of this, I got broken by the next fish, and then lost another. Thinking—blow it, I changed straight back to 26 hook and 10oz line, and I caught two more. Then the whistle went and I knew I had won the King of Clubs—I weighed in four bream for 17lb plus.

Getting back to H/Q, I found that poor Mark Addy thought he had won, as he'd heard that I'd caught nothing, so you can tell how choked he was when he saw my four bream.

I must say that the feeling of winning the King of Clubs was unbelievable. I know the money was very handy but no amount of money makes up for that winning feeling. I do hope to do the double on the King of Clubs one day, as I did in the Pole Championships—we all live in hope!

Before I close, I would like to mention one thing. As a comparison with the King of Clubs, I was also the Chelmer Champion, in 1988. In this match I was catching gudgeon at a nice steady pace, and I was also feeding a few casters across on top of a bed of bloodworm and joker. When I decided to fish across I was after roach—again on a size 26 hook, and a 0.6 line. After a short wait I hooked a 3lb bream—so I put on a piece of extra depth and held the bait still with a big bunch of bloodworm on the hook—and I caught three more bream.

On unhooking the last one, the line broke so I changed my hook length to a 1lb line and a 22 hook to get the fish out more quickly. The water was clear, and I never had another bite for the next half hour. But I knew the fish were still in the swim so after the weigh-in I put the fish back in my net and went back to the same place to fish with 0.6 line and a size 26 hook to see if this worked in the same way as it had done in the King of Clubs. It did—I promptly caught two nice bream, which surely goes to show the importance of light line and small hooks. I've proved this on many occasions, so ... one last tip; use as small hooks as possible, always use floating casters on your hook, and at certain times use floating maggots also. All you need to do to make them float is to put them in a bowl containing $\frac{1}{4}''$ of water for 20 minutes or so, and they should float, and so will counterbalance the weight of the hook—which makes the fish less wary of taking the maggot.

All these little things help to catch a few more fish—and that's what we all go fishing for!

Pat O'Connors Match on the Oxford Canal—by Dickie Carr

Just a short piece to tell you how I made a bad mistake when gudgeon fishing on the Oxford Canal.

I hadn't fished there for a couple of years so when I heard there was a 100 pegger at Kidlington, I decided to have a go, as it was a gudgeon match if you had no cover on the far bank.

I drew peg 19 which was a long walk as it was a split section with three pegs above the lock and seven below; the best three were these above the lock. It was a very good day, and I started off by catching a few gudgeon. I was fishing with the typical gudgeon rig mentioned earlier—but I will first tell you about my feeding pattern. At the start I fed three balls of Damp Leem, with a very small piece of soaked, crushed hemp and joker, the size of a ten pence piece. I fished over the top of this starting to catch gudgeon well. With no more feeding, I caught steadily for $1\frac{1}{2}$ hours. Then they slowed up, so I decided to feed one more small ball, this time the size of a five pence piece. In it went; after ten minutes or so the fish really responded, and I thought 'That's right; you've done the right thing there, Dickie. Keep going'. $1\frac{1}{2}$ hours later, it had slowed up again. I already had about $4\frac{1}{2}$lb of fish in the net; you need about 6lb to get in the frame, I thought. Dare I feed again—because it's funny how easily you can overfeed gudgeon. I was catching, but not fast enough, so, blow it, in went one more ball the size of a 5p piece—and I didn't get another bite! What a mistake.

I weighed in 4lb 9oz and for sixth place was 4lb 15oz. I lost my section by 1oz. I was 6oz out of frame—and I would have caught another 12oz at least if I had not fed again. By the way, I could not even catch on joker after that.

All in all, I only fed less than $\frac{1}{4}$ pint of jokers, yet I definitely put too much in; that's one mistake I hope I don't make again. You never stop learning at this game.

Dickie Carr's Open Match Record, 1979–83

Date	Venue	Place	Method	Weight
(1979)				
14. 5.79	Benson & Hedges, R. Erne, N. Ireland	3rd	Pole	95lb 7oz
15. 5.79	England versus Ireland International (R. Erne system)	1st	Pole	77lb
18. 5.79	Benson & Hedges (Team event)	1st	Pole	
20. 6.79	Brookfield Lane Lake	1st	Waggler	12lb 9oz
27. 6.79	Brookfield Lane Lake	1st	Waggler	13lb 1oz
5. 8.79	R. Thames, Canbury Gardens	2nd	Pole	3lb 1oz
19. 8.79	Dartford Lake, Kent	2nd	Pole	10lb 10oz
29. 8.79	South England Pole Championship (River Lea, Broxbourne)	3rd	Pole	5lb 15oz
19. 9.79	Top 20 North v. South v. Midlands (River Avon, Evesham)	2nd	Waggler	14lb 3oz
17.10.79	Top 20 North v. South v. Midlands (River Lea, Waltham Abbey)	2nd	Waggler	7lb 12oz
28.10.79	River Lea, Broxbourne	1st	Waggler	12lb 8oz
17.11.79	Reading Promenade, River Thames	2nd	Waggler	8lb 11oz
1.12.79	Brookfield Lane Lake	2nd	Bomb	12lb 4oz
9.12.79	River Lea, Broxbourne	2nd	Waggler	4lb 14oz
12.12.79	River Lea, Broxbourne	1st	Feeder	4lb 11oz
13. 1.80	River Ouse, St. Neots	2nd	Waggler	2lb 11oz
26. 1.80	River Lea, St. Margarets	1st	Pole	5lb 1oz
	Top 20, 3rd Overall. 6 wins			
(1980)				
17. 6.80	River Lea, Broxbourne	1st	Waggler	7lb
24. 6.80	Upshire Lake	1st	Pole	11lb 5oz
28. 6.80	Longleat, Sankey Invitation	1st	Waggler	50lb 3oz
5. 7.80	Upshire Lake	3rd	Pole	28lb 8oz
20. 7.80	River Ouse, St. Ives	3rd	Waggler	6lb 5oz
29. 7.80	River Lea, Broxbourne	2nd	Waggler	4lb 9oz
12. 8.80	River Lea, Broxbourne	1st	Waggler	6lb 11oz
17. 8.80	River Lea, Cheshunt	1st	Pole	4lb 12oz
27. 8.80	Coombe Abbey Lake, ABU Invitation	1st	Bomb	27lb 14oz
11. 9.80	BBC TV 'Hooked' Final	2nd	Pole	3lb 15oz
13. 9.80	River Lea, Cheshunt	1st	Pole	4lb 15oz
11.10.80	River Lea, Cheshunt	1st	Pole	3lb 14oz
19.10.80	Thames Evening News, Champion of Champions	2nd	Stick Float	1lb 14oz
29.10.80	River Lea, Broxbourne	3rd	Waggler	6lb 9oz
12.11.80	River Lea, Broxbourne	2nd	Waggler	4lb 15oz
13.12.80	River Lea, Cheshunt	1st	Pole	4lb 12oz
16.12.80	Fishers Green Lake	2nd	Pole	4lb 13oz
28.12.80	River Lea, Tottenham Lock	1st	Pole	8lb 14oz
30.12.80	River Lea, Cheshunt	2nd	Pole	6oz 4drms

Date	Venue	Place	Method	Weight
17. 1.81	Grand Union Canal, Rickmansworth	1st	Pole	4lb 12oz
1. 2.81	River Lea, Tottenham Lock	3rd	Pole	2lb 8oz
7. 2.81	Brookfield Lane Lake	2nd	Bomb	9lb

1st in Lea Valley Winter League, 35 points out of 36.
One of three joint winners of the Southern Top 20, lost on weight.
11 Wins, 57 times in money.

(1981)

4. 4.81	Craigavon Shield:			
	RIVER BANN RECORD	1st	Pole	155lb
	Day 2	2nd	Pole	107lb
17. 5.81	Fermanagh Festival, River Erne	1st	Pole	112lb
21. 5.81	Fermanagh 'Grand Final', River Erne			
	system	2nd	Pole	116lb
20. 6.81	River Ouse, St. Neots	1st	Waggler	4lb 5oz
21. 6.81	London Colney Lakes	1st	Pole	15lb 3oz
28. 6.81	Summer League, Royal Military Canal	3rd	Pole	5lb 5oz
4. 7.81	River Ivel, Pairs Championship	1st	Pole	7lb 12oz
15. 7.81	Brookfield Lane Lake	3rd	Pole	7lb 6oz
19. 7.81	Spade Oak Lake	2nd	Pole	6lb 2oz
22. 7.81	Coombe Abbey Lake, Stamford Carpet	2nd	Bomb	41lb 14oz
	Invitation			
26. 7.81	Summer League, Iden Lock, River	2nd	Waggler	10lb 14oz
	Rother			
5. 8.81	Brookfield Lane Lake	1st	Pole	13lb 10oz
12. 8.81	Brookfield Lane Lake	3rd	Pole	8lb 14oz
4. 9.81	Lea Winter League, River Lea	3rd	Pole	1lb 4oz
15.11.81	Lea Valley Winter League	2nd	Pole	3lb 8oz
14.11.81	River Lea, Tottenham Lock	2nd	Pole	3lb 8oz
29.11.81	Angling Times Winter League	3rd	Pole	2lb 13oz
	(Felmersham, River Ouse)			
5.12.81	Brookfield Lane Lake	2nd	Pole &	5lb 3oz
			Bomb	
12.12.81	River Lea, St. Margarets	1st	Pole	6lb 8oz
10. 1.82	River Lea, Tottenham Lock	1st	Pole	0lb 14oz
31. 1.82	Winter League, Individual Points	2nd		
	Championship			
7. 2.82	River Loddon, Paris Match	1st	Pole	
10. 3.82	River Lea, Cheshunt	2nd	Pole	6lb 9oz
13. 3.82	River Lea, Cheshunt	2nd	Pole	4lb 13oz 8drms
14. 3.82	Oxford Canal	3rd	Pole	2lb 9oz 8drms

9 wins, 46 times in money

(1982)

27/28.				
3.82	R. Bann, Portadown, Ireland	2nd	Pole	52lb
		team	Pole	78lb
26. 5.82	Erne system, Enniskillen Ireland	1st	Pole	10lb 8oz

Date	Venue	Place	Method	Weight
20. 6.82	London Colney Lakes	3rd	Pole	4lb 2oz
27. 6.82	River Lea, Broxbourne	2nd	Pole	4lb 2oz 8drms
12. 7.82	River Lea, Tottenham	1st	Pole	2lb 6oz 8drms
17. 7.82	R. Thames, Wolesly	2nd	Waggler	12lb 5oz
19. 7.82	R. Lea, Tottenham	1st	Pole	3lb 5oz
24. 7.82	Rudyard Lake	2nd Ind 1st team	Pole	6lb 7oz 4drms
25. 7.82	Rudyard Lake	5th	Pole	16lb 14oz 14drms
26. 7.82	R. Lea, Enfield Lock N.V.S. Match	2nd	Pole	11lb 2oz
4. 8.82	Bishops Stortford Lakes, Home Internationals	1st	Pole	17lb 12oz
14. 8.82	Edgbaston Res., Birmingham	4th	Pole	2lb 6oz
21. 8.82	Grand Union Canal, Watford	2nd	Pole	3lb 14oz
12. 9.82	Erne System, Ireland	3rd	Swim-feeder	29lb 7oz
26. 9.82	R. Lea Championship	1st	Pole	6lb 12oz 12drms
16.10.82	R. Lea, Cheshunt	1st	Pole	4lb 2oz
19.10.82	R. Lea, Broxbourne	2nd	Pole	5lb 6oz
24.10.82	Captain Morgan Final R. Bann, N. Ireland	5th 2nd team	Waggler	58lb 9oz
30.10.82	R. Lea, Cheshunt	1st	Pole	31lb 1oz 8drms
31.10.82	R. Ouse, St. Ives	1st team	Waggler	4lb 1oz 8drms
7.11.82	S. Ockenden Carp Fishery	1st	Pole	2lb 2oz
13.11.82	R. Lea, Tottenham	2nd	Waggler	4lb 12oz
20.11.82	R. Lea, Cheshunt	1st	Pole	7oz 8drms
21.11.82	R. Lea, Tottenham	1st	Pole	1lb 5oz 8drms
14.12.82	R. Lea, Fishers Green	3rd	Pole	2lb 13oz
27.12.82	R. Lea, Tottenham	1st	Pole	2lb 7oz 8drms
8. 1.83	R. Lea, Broxbourne	1st	Pole	5lb 8oz
9. 1.83	R. Ouse, Newport Pagnell	2nd	Pole	3lb 10oz 8drms
15. 1.83	R. Lea, St. Margarets	2nd	Pole	9lb 5oz 8drms
16. 1.83	R. Lea, Cheshunt	1st	Pole	3lb 14oz
5. 2.83	R. Lea, St. Margarets	3rd	Pole	5lb 9oz
13. 2.83	R. Lea, Tottenham	3rd team	Pole	2lb 8oz
19. 2.83	R. Lea, St. Margarets	1st	Pole	5lb 14oz
20. 2.83	R. Lea, St. Margarets	3rd	Pole	2lb 11oz

16 wins

(*1983*)

Date	Venue	Place	Method	Weight
22. 5.83	Erne system, Enniskillen, N. Ireland	2nd	Pole	160lb
25. 5.83	Erne system, Enniskillen, N. Ireland (3 day match)	3rd	Pole	total out 280lb
26. 5.83	Final, Erne system, Enniskillen, N.I.	4th	Pole	101lb 8oz
4. 6.83	Aver Lake, S. Ireland	2nd	Pole/ Waggler	31lb
5. 6.83	Aver Lake, S. Ireland (Pairs)	2nd Pair	Pole	28lb

Date	Venue	Place	Method	Weight
8. 6.83	King of Clubs, S. Ireland	4th sec.	Pole	13lb
–11th	4 days	8th sec.	Pole	11lb 8oz
	(3rd Overall with 17 points)	5th sec.	Waggler/	
			slider	17lb 8oz
19. 6.83	London Colney Lakes	3rd	Pole	2lb 7oz 8drms
21. 6.83	R. Lea, Broxbourne	2nd	Pole	1lb 2oz
26. 6.83	R. Lea, Cheshunt	1st	Pole	1lb 14oz 8drms
29. 6.83	London Colney Lakes	1st	Pole	6lb 7oz
3. 7.83	Home International, Newry Canal, Ireland	1st	Pole	27lb 9oz
17. 7.83	Clive Smith Memorial, Gloucester Canal	1st team (England)	Pole	2lb 7oz
31. 7.83	Spake Oak Lake	3rd	Pole	8lb 7oz
25. 9.83	Basingstoke Lake	1st	Pole	7lb 11oz 8drms
2.10.83	Stanborough Lake	1st	Pole	27lb 14oz
22.10.83	River Lea, Tottenham	1st	Pole & Waggler	7lb 1oz 4drms
5.11.83	River Lea, St. Margarets	2nd	Pole	7lb 11oz 8drms
19.11.83		4th	Pole	5lb 8oz 8drms
13.12.83	R. Lea, Fishers Green	4th	Pole	4lb 15oz 8drms
28.12.83	R. Lea, Cooks Ferry Inn	2nd	Pole	2lb 14oz
1. 1.84	R. Lea, Tottenham	2nd	Pole	4lb 12oz
15. 1.84	R. Lea, Cheshunt	1st	Pole	13oz 8drms
21. 1.84	R. Lea, St. Margarets	5th	Pole	5lb
29. 1.84	R. Lea, Tottenham	1st	Pole	5lb 2oz
1. 2.84	G.U. Canal, Watford	2nd	Feeder	2lb 7oz 8drms
5. 2.84	Ardleigh Reservoir	5th	Bomb	3lb 3oz 12drms
11. 2.84	R. Lea, St. Margarets	1st	Pole	6lb 14oz 4drms
12. 2.84	G.U.C. Southall	4th	Pole	3lb 11oz 4drms
15. 2.84	G.U.C. Southall	5th	Pole	15oz 4drms
3. 3.84	R. Lea, Cooks Ferry Inn	1st	Pole	6lb 8oz
10. 3.84	R. Lea, Tottenham	5th	Pole	21lb 8oz

11 wins

(*1984*)

Date	Venue	Place	Method	Weight
27. 6.84	R. Lea, Ponders End	2nd	Pole	1lb 8oz 8drms
30. 6.84	Newey Ind Match	5th	Pole	23lb 8oz
1. 7.84	Ireland Team Match	1st	Pole	17lb 3oz
5. 7.84	R. Lea, Cooks Ferry	3rd	Pole	1lb 13oz 8drms
21. 7.84	National Championship G.U.C. London	1st sec. 5th overall	Pole	7lb 5oz
25. 7.84	R. Lee, Ponders End	3rd	Pole	3lb 5oz 8drms
4. 8.84	Kings Cross, Regent Canal	2nd	Pole	7lb 12oz
12. 8.84	Spake Oak Lake	3rd	Pole	4lb 9oz
18. 8.84	R. Lea, Tottenham	4th	Pole	5lb 15oz 8drms
22. 8.84	T/V Classic, Holme Pierrepont, Nottingham	2nd	Feeder	19lb 6oz 8drms

Date	Venue	Place	Method	Weight
26. 8.84	Home International, Ireland	1st sec.	Waggler	16lb 6oz
		1st team		28lb 3oz
7. 9.84	Balybay 2 days, Ireland	3rd one		
		day	Feeder	63lb 2oz
8. 9.84	Balybay 2 days, Ireland	6th over 2 days		
14. 9.84 to	Ireland Bass	1st overall		72lb 8oz
18. 9.84	Ireland Bass	2nd overall		102lb 7oz
	winner of Bass over 3 days, £1,600 winnings			
6.10.84	King's Cross, Regent Canal	4th	Pole	4lb 4oz 8drms
10.11.84	Ireland, Portadown Bann	1st sec.		40lb
11.11.84	Ireland, Portadown Bann	2nd overall 2 days		140lb
25.11.84	South Ockendon Lake	1st	Pole	5lb 8oz 8drms
4.12.84	R. Lea, Fishers Green	2nd	Pole	6lb 15oz 8drms
15.12.84	R. Lea, Broxbourne	1st	Pole	10lb 8drms
5. 1.84	Chelmsford Chelmer	2nd	Pole	4lb 11oz
13. 1.85	R. Lea, Fishers Green (pairs match)	1st pairs		4lb 6oz
27. 1.85	R. Lea, Tottenham	1st	Pole	2lb 5oz 12drms
10. 2.85	R. Lea, Tottenham	2nd	Pole	7oz 8drms
20. 2.85	R. Lea, St. Margarets	1st	Pole	10lb 5oz
27. 2.85	R. Lea, St. Margarets	4th	Pole	8lb 5oz
2. 3.85	Southall G.U.C.	1st	Waggler	6lb 9oz
3. 3.85	South Ockendon Lake	2nd	Pole	5lb 2oz
13. 3.85	R. Lea, St. Margarets	3rd	Pole	6lb 1oz
	9 wins			

(*1985*)

Date	Venue	Place	Method	Weight
11. 5.85 to	Enniskillen Erne system,Ireland	2nd	Pole	45lb 7oz
		3rd	Pole	70lb 8oz
9. 6.85		2nd	Pole	99lb 1oz

KING OF CLUBS (4th overall, 17 points)—3 day

Date	Venue	Place	Method	Weight
23. 6.85	R. Lea, Tottenham	5th	Pole	5lb 13oz
26. 6.85	R. Lea, Ponders End	2nd	Pole	2lb 11oz 4drms
24. 6.85	Upshire Lake	1st	Waggler	47lb
30. 6.85	Spake Oak Lake	1st	Pole	6lb 5oz 5drms
2. 7.85	Kings Cross, Regent Canal	1st	Pole	3lb 7oz
7. 7.85	Newrey Canal, Ireland	3rd	Pole	15lb 1oz
9. 7.85	Kings Cross, Regent Canal	1st	Pole	4lb 9oz 8drms
13. 7.85	Kings Cross, Regent Canal	1st	Pole	5lb 2oz 8drms
14. 7.85	Watford G.U.C.	3rd	Pole	5lb 9oz
16. 7.85	Kings Cross, Regent Canal	1st	Pole	3lb 12oz 8drms
20. 7.85	National Leeds & Liverpool	1st team		
23. 7.85	Kings Cross, Regent Canal	1st	Waggler	4lb 5oz
25. 7.85	R. Lea, Cockfosters	3rd	Pole	3lb 9oz 8drms

Date	Venue	Place	Method	Weight
4. 8.85	Hanger Lane, G.U.C.	1st	Pole	7lb 6oz 8drms
5. 8.85	R. Lea, Hereford	1st	Pole	3lb 1oz
8. 8.85	Cooks Ferry Inn	2nd	Pole	3lb 9oz 4drms
11. 2.85	Southall G.U.C.	3rd	Pole	8lb 8drms
14. 8.85	Brookfield Lane	2nd	Waggler	11lb 12oz
15. 9.85	South Ockenden Lake	1st	Pole	9lb
21. 9.85	Leyland Thames	3rd	Pole	11lb 5oz
22. 9.85	Mapel Drain	3rd	Pole	6lb 2oz
24. 9.85	Oxford Canal	2nd	Pole	6lb 12drms
5.10.85	Brookfield Lake	4th	Pole	8lb 5oz
13.10.85	South Ockenden Lake	1st	Pole	10lb 5oz
9.11.85	British Pole Championship, Nottingstow	1st in Final		2lb 4oz
10.11.85	South Ockendon Lake	1st	Pole	7lb 10oz
3.12.85	R. Lee, Fishers Green	3rd	Pole	2lb 14oz 8drms
14.12.85	Hanger Lane, G.U.C.	1st	Pole	8lb 12oz 4drms
15.12.85	R. Lea, Tottenham	3rd	Pole	6lb 10oz 6drms
31.12.85	R. Lea, St. Margarets	1st	Pole	8lb 10oz
4. 1.86	R. Lea, Cockfosters	2nd	Pole	3lb 3oz
11. 1.86	R. Lea, Cockfosters	2nd	Pole	8lb 8oz
5. 2.86	R. Lea, Cockfosters	3rd	Pole	3lb 1oz 8drms
8. 2.86	R. Lea, Cockfosters	5th	Pole	1lb 3oz
9. 2.86	Oxford Canal	5th in League over six matches		
15. 2.86	Hanger Lane, G.U.C.	4th	Pole	4oz 4drms
19. 2.86	R. Lea, St. Margarets	1st	Pole	9lb 5oz 8drms
12. 3.86	R. Lea, St. Margarets (The Lord Louis)	1st	Pole	10lb 2oz

18 wins

(*1986*)

Date	Venue	Place	Method	Weight
29. 3.86	Portadown, Ireland	2nd	Pole	100lb 15oz
30. 3.86	Portdown, Ireland	2nd	Pole	128lb 7oz
31. 3.86	Portadown, Ireland	(2nd Overall over 2 days match)		
		2nd	Pole	79lb
15. 5.86	Ireland, Enniskillen	4th	Pole	21lb 2oz
18. 5.86	Dublin	4th	Pole	2oz 12drms
19. 5.86	Ireland, Enniskillen	1st	Feeder	93lb
22. 5.86 to 23. 5.86	Enre Bait Festival	2nd final Feeder		89lb 7oz
25. 5.86	Southern Ireland	3rd	Pole	5lb 14oz
29. 5.86	Enniskillen Festival, Ireland	2nd	Pole	74lb
30. 5.86	Enniskillen Festival, Ireland	3rd in Final		99lb
4. 5.86	Carrick on Shannon King of Clubs	1st		57lb 8oz
5. 5.86	Carrick on Shannon King of Clubs	4th		5lb 15oz

Date	Venue	Place	Method	Weight
6. 5.86	Carrick on Shannon King of Clubs	2nd		19lb 7oz

(1st Overall 146 out of 150) (won £6,818 in 4 weeks)

Date	Venue	Place	Method	Weight
23. 6.86	Hertford, River Lea	2nd	Pole	3lb 7oz 4drms
24. 6.86	R. Lea, Broxbourne	3rd	Waggler	1lb 15oz 4drms
19. 7.86	R. Lea, Tottenham	3rd	Pole	6lb 6oz 8drms
9. 8.86	Long Melford Sport	1st	Pole	12lb 5oz
20. 8.86	White Bread League	8th over 4 matches		
23. 8.86	Southall G.U.C.	1st	Pole	15lb
				(Record for venue
25. 8.86	R. Lea, Ponders End	2nd	Pole	3lb 5oz
11.10.86	R. Lea, Tottenham	2nd	Pole	8lb 4oz 12drms
23.11.86	Slapton G.U.C.	5th	Waggler	3lb 6oz 8drms
6.12.86	Southall G.U.C.	1st	Pole	3lb 4oz
13.12.86	R. Lea, Cheshunt	4th	Pole	7oz 8drms
16.12.86	R. Lea, Fishers Green	3rd	Pole	1lb 4oz
17.12.86	Hanger Lane, G.U.C.	3rd	Pole	4lb 4oz
31.12.86	R. Lea, Enfield Lock	4th	Pole	3lb 1oz
10. 1.87	R. Lea, Cooks Ferry Inn	1st	Pole	8lb 9oz 8drms
15. 1.87	Harefield, G.U.C.	4th	Waggler	2lb 6oz 8drms
4. 2.87	Mainstone Res.	4th	Bomb	15oz
7. 2.87	Long Melford	5th	Pole	6lb 2oz
14. 2.87	Kingsland Road, E.1	5th	Pole	4lb 10oz
15. 2.87	Kings Cross	4th	Pole	3lb 4oz 8drms
18. 2.87	Kingsland Road, E.1	5th	Pole	3lb 4oz 12drms
28. 2.87	Richmond Thames	5th	Stilt	21lb
4. 3.87	Richmond Thames	Top 20. Winner over 10 match		
12. 3.87	Kingsland Road, E.1	1st	Pole	3lb 13oz 8drms

9 wins

(*1987*)

Date	Venue	Place	Method	Weight
8. 5.87	Southern Ireland	1st	Bomb	22lb 14oz
11. 5.87	Enniskillen, Ireland	2nd	Bomb	25lb 8oz
27. 5.87	Enniskillen, Ireland	3rd	Waggler	24lb 6oz
21. 6.87	F. Stratford, G.U.C.	3rd	Pole	7lb 5oz
22. 6.87	R. Lea, St. Margarets	2nd	Pole	1lb 8drms
25. 6.87	R. Lea, Cooks Ferry	1st	Pole	8lb 9oz
28. 6.87	R. Lea, Tottenham	1st	Pole	13lb 0oz
5. 7.87	Alesdury Arm	3rd	Pole	5lb 15oz
6. 7.87	Cooks Ferry Inn	1st	Pole	3lb 6oz
9. 7.87	Cooks Ferry Inn	4th	Pole	3lb 5oz
11. 7.87	Greenford Lake	2nd	Pole	11lb 8drms
13. 7.87	R. Lea, Cooks Ferry Inn	3rd	Pole	3lb 4oz
15. 7.87	R. Lea, Ponders End	2nd	Pole	3lb 14oz
18. 7.87	R. Lea, Tottenham	4th	Pole	10lb 4oz
19. 7.87	R. Lea, Waltham Abbey	2nd	Pole	13lb 9oz

Date	Venue	Place	Method	Weight
23. 7.87	R. Lea, Cooks Ferry Inn	3rd	Pole	4lb 9oz
29. 7.87	Hatfield Forest Lake	1st	Pole	5lb 13oz 4drms
1. 8.87	Ipswich Lake	1st	Pole	10lb 10oz 8drms
7. 9.87	Dunnconraft, S. Ireland	3rd	Pole	4lb 9oz 8drms
8. 9.87	Dunnconraft, S. Ireland	4th	Waggler	6lb 10oz
9. 9.87	Dunnconraft, S. Ireland	6th	Pole	4lb 10oz
10. 9.87	Dunnconraft, S. Ireland	6th	Waggler	3lb 8oz
9. 9.87	Dunnconraft, S. Ireland	6th	Pole	4–100
10. 9.87	Dunnconraft, S. Ireland	6th	Waggler	3–800
3.10.87	Fishers Green	4th	Pole	5lb 6oz
11.10.87	Milton Keynes, G.U.C.	2nd	Waggler	5lb 12oz 8drms
14.10.87	Lady Capel, G.U.C.	1st	Bomb	21lb 5oz
17.10.87	Bankside, G.U.C.	2nd	Pole	3lb 5oz 8drms
7.11.87	Mile End, G.U.C.	2nd	Pole	14oz
29.11.87	R. Lea, Tottenham	2nd	Pole	7lb 6oz
3.12.87	R. Lea, Enfield	3rd	Pole	4lb 5oz
5.12.87	Southall, G.U.C.	1st	Waggler	6lb 10oz
6.12.87	R. Lea, Tottenham	1st	Pole	7lb 15oz 8drms
20.12.87	Enfield Pairs Match	3rd	Pole	6lb 4drms
2. 1.88	R. Lea, Waltham Abbey	2nd	Pole	7lb 13oz
9. 1.88	R. Lea, Cooks Ferry	3rd	Pole	6lb 13oz
27. 2.88	Kingsland Road, G.U.C.	1st	Pole	4lb 7oz

10 wins

(*1988*)

Date	Venue	Place	Method	Weight
5. 5.88	Bally Bay, S. Ireland	1st	Bomb	18lb 4oz
22. 5.88	Enniskillen, Ireland	1st	Bomb	24lb 6oz
27. 5.88	Enniskillen, Ireland	1st	Bomb	30lb 7oz
16. 6.88	R. Lea, Cooks Ferry	3rd	Pole	3lb 2oz
13. 7.88	L/Colney Lake	2nd	Pole	2lb 14oz
17. 7.88	Upminster Lake	4th	Pole	4lb 2oz
23. 7.88	Farnborough Lake	2nd	Pole	16lb 9oz
26. 7.88	R. Lea, Waltham Abbey	2nd	Pole & Waggler	2lb 5oz
4. 9.88	Pole Champ Final, Glos	1st	Pole	12lb 14oz
6. 9.88 ⎫ 7. 9.88 ⎬ Enniskillen, Ireland 8. 9.88 ⎭		2nd		30lb 12oz
2.10.88	Paddock Wood Lake	1st	Pole	15lb 5oz
16.10.88	Fished for England	1st team	Pole	2oz
19.10.88	Basingstoke Canal	3rd	Pole	6lb 15oz
29.10.88	R. Lea, St. Margarets	2nd	Pole	7lb 4oz
30.10.88	Layer Pit	1st	Pole	6lb 6oz
9.11.88	Welwyn Garden City	1st	Pole & Bomb	14lb 11oz
13.11.88	Chemper Champ	1st	Pole	18lb 3oz
1. 1.89	R. Lea, Broxbourne	3rd	Waggler	2lb 2oz

Date	Venue	Place	Method	Weight
15. 1.89	R. Lea, Broxbourne	4th	Waggler	1lb 15oz
22. 1.89	White Hard, Wey	2nd	Pole	3lb 1oz
18. 2.89	Coxley Moor, G.U.C.	3rd	Pole	6lb 10oz
	9 wins			

(*1989*)

6. 5.89	Enniskillen, Ireland			
	P&O			
10. 5.89				
to		3rd	Pole	19lb 6oz
12. 5.89	(5th Overall of Week Festival)			
19. 5.89	Enre Bait Festival		Pole	25lb
26. 5.89	B&I Festival (Places in Final) (Places in Final)		Feeder	33lb 7oz
9. 7.89	Basingstoke Team Championship	1st team	Pole	1lb 14oz 8drms
	Basingstoke Canal			
19. 7.89	R. Lea, Enfield Lock	1st	Pole	3lb 2oz
5. 8.89	R. Lea, Tottenham	1st	Pole	7lb 6oz
6. 8.89	Kirkstead, Witham	4th	Pole	7lb 14oz
27. 8.89	Stillwater Lake	2nd	Waggler	10lb 10oz
28. 8.89	Willow Park (2 day)	2nd	Pole	18lb 8oz
	(Winner of 2 day Festival)			
2. 9.89	Enniskillen, Ireland	1st	Feeder	62lb 14oz
to		unplaced		8lb 2oz
6. 9.89				
7. 9.89	Bass Festival	4th	Feeder	41lb 4oz
to				
8. 9.89				
	(2nd Overall in Bass Festival)			
13. 9.89	Cavan	2nd sec.	Feeder	40lb 14oz
15. 9.89	King of Clubs	4th sec.	Waggler	9lb 2oz
16. 9.89	King of Clubs	10th sec.	Pole	14lb 12oz
	(10th in King of Clubs)			
7.10.89	Southampton	2nd	Pole	5lb 8oz
8.10.89	Northampton, G.U.C.	4th	Pole	4lb 7oz 8drms
11.10.89	Farnborough, Basingstoke Canal	5th	Pole	4lb 10oz 6drms
15.10.89	Lea Team Championship	1st team	Pole	6lb 12oz
21.10.89	Kingsland Road, E.1	4th	Pole	6lb 13oz
5.11.89	White Hart, Wey, Nav. Canal	1st	Pole	3lb 13oz
11.11.89	Gosfield Lake	2nd	Pole	12lb 6oz
26.11.89	Oxford Canal	1st	Pole	7lb 1oz 8drms
29.11.89	W. Garden City, Stanborough Lake	3rd	Pole	5lb 14oz
3.12.89	Ireland	1st sec.	Pole	100lb 4oz
4.12.89	Lower Bann	1st sec.	Waggler	69lb 14oz
	Anglers World Festival	7th Overall		
13.12.89	W. Garden City, Stanborough Lake	3rd	Pole	5lb 5oz 8drms

Date	Venue	Place	Method	Weight	
24.12.89	Ladbrook Grove, W.11, G.U.C.	3rd	Waggler	6lb	8oz
7. 1.90	F/Stratford, G.U.C.	5th	Pole	6lb	7oz
10. 1.90	Victy Park, E.1, Regent Canal	2nd	Waggler	9lb	7oz
14. 1.90	R. Lea, Cheshunt	1st	Pole	8lb	1oz
31. 1.90	W. Garden City, Stanborough Lake	1st	Pole	12lb	6oz
10. 3.90	Ponders End, R. Lea	2nd	Waggler	9lb	2oz

FISHED 6 FESTIVALS IN IRELAND, PLACES IN ALL 6.

World Championship Results

Year and venue		Teams		Points
1957	Belgrade (Yugoslavia)	1.	Italy	23
		2.	Luxembourg	32
		3.	France	43
1958	Huy (Belgium)	1.	Belgium	29
		2.	France	32
		3.	Luxembourg	86
1959	Neuchatel (Switzerland)	1.	France	71
		2.	Italy	96
		3.	Switzerland	105
1960	Gdansk (Poland)	1.	Belgium	36
		2.	France	61
		3.	E. Germany	87
1961	Mersebourg (E. Germany)	1.	E. Germany	44
		2.	Belgium	66
		3.	England	70
1962	Lake Garda (Italy)	1.	Italy	24
		2.	France	71
		3.	Belgium	95
1963	Wormeldange (Luxembourg)	1.	France	57
		2.	Italy	77
		3.	England	80
1964	Isola Pescaroli (Italy)	1.	France	6
		2.	Italy	19
		3.	Austria	20
1965	Galati (Romania)	1.	Romania	22
		2.	France	27
		3.	Poland	32
1966	River Thurne (England)	1.	France	11
		2.	Belgium	15
		3.	Italy	24
1967	Dunajvaros (Yugoslavia)	1.	Belgium	12
		2.	France	17
		3.	England	25
1968	Fermoy (Irish Republic)	1.	France	18
		2.	W. Germany	24
		3.	Roumania	25
1969	Bad Oldeslow (W. Germany)	1.	Holland	17
		2.	Belgium	19
		3.	France	21
1970	Berg (Holland)	1.	Belgium	8
		2.	Holland	14
		3.	France	16
1971	Peschiera (Italy)	1.	Italy	6
		2.	Belgium	21
		3.	France	25
1972	Prague (Czechoslovakia)	1.	France	12
		2.	England	24
		3.	Italy	25

1973	Chalon-sur-Saone (France)	1.	Belgium	16
		2.	France	26
		3.	England	28
1974	Ghent (Belgium)	1.	France	18
		2.	Italy	18
		3.	Holland	21
1975	Bydgoszcz (Poland)	1.	France	23
		2.	England	26
		3.	Belgium	26
1976	Varna (Bulgaria)	1.	Italy	7
		2.	Bulgaria	20
		3.	Austria	27
1977	Ehenen (Luxembourg)	1.	Luxembourg	16
		2.	Belgium	18
		3.	France	19
1978	Vienna (Austria)	1.	France	14
		2.	Italy	19
		3.	Czechoslovakia	24
1979	Zarag (Spain)	1.	France	14
		2.	Holland	16
		3.	Portugal	24
1980	Mannheim (W. Germany)	1.	Germany	7
		2.	England	23
		3.	Belgium	24
1981	Luddington (England)	1.	France	25
		2.	England	31
		3.	Wales	37
1982	Newry Canal (Ireland)	1.	Holland	20
		2.	France	25
		3.	England	26
1983	Rijnkanaal, Piel (Holland)	1.	Belgium	9
		2.	England	14
		3.	Holland	24
1984	Switzerland, River Thielle	1.	Luxembourg	28 (on weight)
		2.	England	28
		3.	Belgium	40
1985	Italy, River Arno	1.	England	16
		2.	Italy	17
		3.	Belgium	25
1986	France, Strasbourg	1.	Italy	27 (on weight)
		2.	W. Germany	27
		3.	Austria	40
1987	Portugal, River Mordego	1.	England	9
		2.	Italy	18
		3.	Austria	33
1988	Belgium, Damme Canal	1.	England	50 (on weight)
		2.	Italy	50
		3.	France	58
1989	Bulgaria	1.	Wales	
		2.	Italy	
		3.	England	

Photo Credits

John Baker: 15, 16, 21, 23, 25, 26, 27, 28, 32, 33, 34, 35, 36, 37, 40, 43, 44, 49, 50, 52, 65, 69, 82, 84, 85, 86, 87
Peter Burrell: 108
Rodney Coldron: 9, 97, 105
Kevin Maddocks: 12, 51
Bruce Vaughan: 27, 30, 73, 90, 91, 92, 99
Dave Harper: Front cover, 110
Angling Times: Back cover
Cyril Holbrook: 41, 42